ENDORSEMENTS

It's been a deep joy getting to know Allison over the last few years. I am so inspired by her friendship with God and the deep well of wisdom that flows out of her heart.

It is an incredible thing when an author can write a book that leads you into an encounter with the Author and Finisher of our faith. Allison has done that in this new book: *The Image*.

From the first few paragraphs of this book, I found my heart meeting with the One who is writing my story.

- Jonathan David Helser
Worshipper / Songwriter / Musician

Allison is a joyful mix of thinker and pragmatist—processing the deeper revelations of Christ and yet not satisfied to leave them standing alone in the cold.

Using story, depth of thought and invitation, she challenges our Kingdom journey into new adventures, providing needed tools to reach our destination.

A must-read book for moving your identity into action, fulfilling all the Father has for you.

- Byron Easterling
Build His House Ministries
ByronEasterling.com

I first heard Allison at one of her Ignite conferences and was refreshed by her powerful and practical teaching. Her insight into our spiritual identity served as a catalyst that helped me explore and develop my God-given identity as a father and husband—and gave me tools to work with athletes, coaches, and business leaders.

I have seen the wisdom in this book enable those under my leadership to walk confidently in their New Man identity through some of life's most difficult situations.

These truths have deeply impacted the direction of athletic programs, changed the course of businesses, restored marriages, and given athletes a newfound strength based in who they are, as opposed to how they perform.

Without understanding and experiencing our true identity from God's perspective, the challenges of this world can crush us. *The Image* will help you rest in how God truly sees you, allowing you to love the process of developing your unique identity in Christ.

- Eric Dykstra
Pastor / former regional director with Fellowship of
Christian Athletes

Walking alongside a client is a sacred journey. It requires merging onto the arterial roadway of recovery to reach healing and freedom. I have observed as a therapist that all roads on this journey lead to one key question: "Who am I and how do I see myself?"

In *The Image*, Allison gives the reader a spiritual GPS. Lies are exposed and truth is revealed. This book affirms to my clients that their identity solidly rests in being one who is "accepted in the Beloved."

As a beloved teacher, mentor and friend, Allison has seen in me the image God sees—and now I rest in knowing who I am.

- Faith Donaldson
Psychotherapist / Spiritual Director / Podcaster

When I first met Allison, I knew immediately that she was a kindred spirit. Her passion to set the captives free is contagious. Allison's unique set of gifts will equip and empower you.

As someone who has also taken a stand for social justice, especially in the area of human trafficking, I am thankful for Allison, who understands how identity and freedom go hand in hand. Identity is one of the keys in the kingdom of God and I am honored that she is sharing this key with us.

- Alisha Siemens
Co-Founder / CEO Sharma Global

To hear that God is love and that you are the beloved is a transformational biblical truth. But how do you actually live from that point of view?

At our National Conference, Allison brought such clarity to our identity in Christ. We learned to unmask the lies in our thinking and to live from our relationship with God! The practical application and exercises were excellent. The picture activations shared in this book brought our identity in Christ to a higher level.

Everybody can remember a teacher who had a passion for what they taught and because of that your heart was changed. That's Allison. She speaks with passion and clarity about the love of God for us, radiating His rest and friendliness—an image carrier of Jesus.

- **Phia Kemp**
National President Aglow Netherlands

THE IMAGE

EXPERIENCE LIFE FROM GOD'S PERSPECTIVE

ALLISON BOWN

The Image
Copyright First Edition © 2018
Allison Bown

Designed by Bethel Media
Copyedited by Rebecca Emenaker
Proofreading and typesetting by Printopya

This book and other materials published by Allison Bown are available online at
www.BrilliantBookHouse.com

 BRILLIANT BOOK HOUSE

Published by Brilliant Book House
PO BOX 871450
Vancouver, WA, 98687

Unless otherwise indicated, all Scripture quotation are taken from New King James Version, Amplified Bible Classic Edition, New Living Translation or New American Standard Bible.

ISBN: 978-0-9896262-7-9

For Randy,
my husband, who has eyes that see
who God created me—and us—to be.

And in memory of Isabel,
who now understands how beautiful she always was.

ACKNOWLEDGEMENTS

All of us stand on the shoulders of others who have gone before us. Our journey is better because friends have willingly walked with us and stood by us. I am blessed for this to be the story of my life, but it is especially true in the writing of this book.

There are many voices reflected in these pages—fellow travelers who came to workshops and training days to explore their identity; who have sat with me in living rooms, conference rooms and around fire pits while we discovered more about who God is and who we really are in Him.

Jenny, Theresa, Kelly, Earlene, Rachel, Rick, Gary, Mike, Carol, Stacey, Byron, Crystal, Lucas, my Learning Circle friends and Brilliant companions—you all make me think more radiantly. Your wisdom and kindness in my life have been astonishing. And thanks, Josh, for finding the real title.

Rebecca Emenaker, you took my writing and made it better, always hearing my heart. Sophie, Mark and Danielle at Brilliant Book House—I greatly appreciate who you are and who you've been to me and for me on this journey.

And Randy, my greatest champion of all. Your love, wisdom and grace in my life have transformed me.

This book would not exist without the generosity of my friend and fellow explorer, Graham Cooke. He loves truth so much, he shares it freely and invites us all to take what we hear, explore with Jesus and expand it with what we discover in our own story and journey with God.

His commitment to creating a symphony of believers who are astonished by the magnificence of the gospel is immense. He continues to willingly go first into uncharted territory, and because of that, we travel faster.

I look forward to discovering what lies behind the ranges that we still have yet to see.

CONTENTS

FOREWORD
by Graham Cooke

Allison is my friend and creative partner. Together, and with significant others, we have spent thousands of hours excitedly and joyfully in a Kingdom dialogue that transcends normal, usual life by imagining, dreaming and focusing visually, mentally, emotionally and spiritually on who God is and what He is like for us and to us!

This book is a product of the story that Allison and I have been on individually and in team. It's been a journey of walking these truths through impossible scenarios that have not only produced personal freedom but also created a map for others to follow.

The Father put each of us into Christ so that He could see us in the same way He sees Jesus and relate to us in the same manner as they relate to One another. That is glorious in and of itself. The truly beautiful part occurs when we realize that we can see, imagine, trust and believe that "as He is, so are we in this world" (1 John 4:17).

The first words ever spoken about man in relation to God defined forever the purpose in creating men and women to become the very image of His nature: "Let us make man in Our image, according to our likeness, and let them rule over..." (Genesis 1:26). This is a thrilling concept that provides the same beautiful, relentless context for every circumstance and life lesson known to humankind. We are always lovingly, gently and joyfully being set up by God to find Him and discover ourselves in Him. Regardless of circumstances, He remains the same—always. It is that North Star consistency that makes trusting Him such a powerful and pleasurable experience. He is unchanging.

The Image is all about our identity in Christ. We are a new creation learning to step away from our old pre-cross carnality as we constantly explore the post-resurrection lifestyle of the new man in Jesus. Jesus has already taken the old to the cross, and the grave. It no longer exists in God's perspective. He only sees your resurrected self as the new man in Christ.

There is a divine displacement that must occur as God uses our life events to create a habitational relationship with us. The old man must give way to the new creation in Christ. As a new creation, you step out of and away from the old and step into and toward the real you as God made you in Christ.

This lifestyle is all about elevation. Learning the art of being in Christ means seeing and responding to Him on the higher level of the Kingdom, rather than the ordinary level of world culture and expression.

The Image is structured much like a staircase. It provides us with a multiplicity of keys that guide us step by step to go to a higher place of relationship with God and one another. Along the way, fear is overcome, and with it every negative emotion becomes upgraded to God's image and our new likeness.

There are huge, powerful and delightful upgrades for us to experience—and opportunities to upgrade how you see yourself is in every chapter. Freedom in your new identity will empower you to grow more quickly than you ever thought possible. That is purely because we do not have to work on the old in order to become new!

You will discover the immensity of your freedom in the Lord and your language will grow to express trust, faith, favor and expectation. The currency of your renewed lifestyle is the perspective and the promises of God toward you in Jesus.

Part Two of this astonishing spiritual work is a Guidebook that provides ideas and options to travel in this new territory. The map is drawn from whatever you encounter and allow yourself to become in Jesus.

You will discover landmarks that enable you to know where you are at all times. You will be given questions (until you can find your own!) to enable your exploration.

You will write your own Identity Statement and learn its inherent power to enable overcoming.

You will begin to see, hear and speak out your own Inheritance Words of Destiny.

You will curate your own Evidences of Transformation.

And all along the way, Allison will empower you to create high points of connection between you and the Lord.

FOREWORD

In Brilliant, Allison and I believe that all theology is relational and not merely academic. And, therefore, she uses a relational narrative to empower our thinking and language so that we may discover who God is for us—now.

Allison is particularly excellent in offering real-life examples and practical tools for discovering and unpacking true identity in Jesus. She is both imaginative and pragmatic in her equipping and training.

She loves to upgrade our story and take people on a journey, teaching them to get unstuck, develop a new lens, and overcome all obstacles. She is a cartographer drawing the map as she writes.

This book is a culmination of many years of developing people in identity. The training and tools it contains will empower people to establish a lifestyle of being in Christ. The catalogue of aids to power and significance will expand to overcome everything that is against you.

The antidote to the past is not just the present being upgraded: it is the future being determined and knowing your place in it!

Graham Cooke
Author, speaker and consultant at Brilliant

A PRAYER AS YOU READ

Father,
You alone open the eyes of our hearts to see as You see. Your love opens our ears to hear the resonant sound of Your goodness.

Jesus,
You paid the greatest price to give the Father a family. You revel in being our Friend, though it cost you everything to do so. And now You pray for us continually to discover our life the way You've always imagined it.

Holy Spirit,
Your laughter restores joy to our soul. Your wisdom comforts, heals, and teaches us. Your delight in showing us the true nature of the Father and Son is unparalleled.

All we can say and sing and whisper is "thank You." Thank You for holding the image of who we are when we have forgotten. Thank You for singing our song of life until we can sing it too.

May we become the symphony You deserve, a sound of goodness and grace on earth as it is in heaven, because we've beheld the image of who You really are and, in the process, have become who You've always seen us to truly be.

"The Lord your God in your midst, The Mighty One, will save; He will rejoice over you with gladness, He will quiet you with His love, He will rejoice over you with singing."
Zephaniah 3:17

PROLOGUE

As I sat in my office, I realized once again that I wasn't working—I was staring. What had started out as a minor distraction was becoming an all-consuming focus.

The object of my fascination was a large, 19-by-14 inch, black and white photograph titled *Monolith: The Face of Half Dome*. While most offices don't boast museum-quality art, mine did; a benefit of being the workshop director for a gallery of photography in Yosemite National Park. It was the early 1980s and being surrounded by world-class photographs was a wonderful part of my daily life.

But of all the amazing images on display, this one captivated me in a way that I couldn't quite explain. Was it the pitch-black sky? The sharp contrasts of rock and snow? Or the perspective that captured the massiveness of the unique granite face of Half Dome? I didn't really know. I was simply fascinated—and just kept staring.

Several weeks had gone by when a veteran workshop instructor dropped in for a visit. As we chatted, I commented on the photograph. "You know the story, don't you?" he asked. When I replied that I did not, he broke into a huge grin, the kind that someone has when they're about to give you an amazing present—and he was right. After just a few sentences, I knew why I was so intrigued by this picture. There was a story waiting to be told . . .

. . . the story of an image that didn't exist.

In the winter of 1927, a young man from San Francisco found himself living in Yosemite Valley, enchanted by the possibilities of capturing this magnificent landscape on film—but he was a very frustrated young man. His goal was to photograph one of Yosemite's most iconic landmarks: Half Dome. He wanted a perspective that would communicate what he would later call "a brooding form, with deep shadows and a distant sharp white peak against a dark sky," and made numerous, arduous trips with his mule to the remote vantage point he had selected. Each time, he

19

packed his large 6-by-8 inch view camera and heavy glass plates, only to return with disappointing results after emerging from the darkroom.[i]

Instead of the sheer face of Half Dome dominating the image, it blended into the daytime sky behind it. The gray value of a blue sky and the gray value of this massive rock formation were almost the same in a black and white photograph. The young photographer knew that a midnight-black backdrop would create the contrast needed, but that would, of course, eliminate the light necessary for the photograph.

**So he did something that no one else had done
before: He took a photograph that didn't exist —
except in his imagination.**

He calculated that by placing a red filter over his lens, the blue sky would be transformed into a deep black, finally bringing the granite face of Half Dome to center stage. In underexposing the film by the smallest margin, he could preserve the detail in the snow. Even then, the photograph would require extensive work in the darkroom to bring to life the image that he felt with his heart as much as he imagined in his mind.

It wasn't a quick process, but each darkroom session taught him something that he hadn't considered before. He invented new ways to do things and broke most of the standing rules of photography to do so. In the end, he emerged with an image on paper that was exactly as he had visualized it before he ever snapped the shutter. It would become one of the most valuable photographs in history and launched a new era in photographic art. It was a masterpiece that Ansel Adams titled *Monolith: The Face of Half Dome.*

My friend smiled once again. It had indeed been a good story, but I had no idea of the deposit that God had just made into my spirit about His higher ways. Father God often delights in hiding spiritual truth in the fabric of the world around us. For many years that deposit lay dormant in my heart, waiting to spring to life.

It wasn't until the mid-1990s, during a season that could aptly be described as both the best and worst of times, that I discovered a small copy of my beloved *Monolith* buried in a box. Once again, the story began to stir in my spirit. It was a season when my own identity and destiny felt as if it were being randomly swirled about in God's great darkroom, leaving me with little clue of who I really was and who He saw me to actually be.

At the time, I was tentatively holding on to the truth that before my days on earth ever began, God knew who He had created me to be. He told Jeremiah that He had set him apart before he was born (Jeremiah 1:5). In Psalm 139:16, David wrote that "Your eyes saw my substance, being yet unformed. And in Your book they all were written, the days fashioned for me, when as yet there were none of them." God had already envisioned my life before I was ever born.

But how did God imagine my life to be? What was the image of me that He saw? And how could I see myself that way on earth?

As I contemplated the story that I had heard years before, the Holy Spirit smiled— and began to unwrap how His ways were so like the photograph I adored.

God could see my identity clearly, but there was a process of development until I could see myself from His perspective.

Even though the current circumstances of my life left me unclear about my future, could it be that this was exactly the process of development I needed to become who God had always seen me to be? Was it possible that while my familiar religious rule book appeared to be evaporating, His truth was coming into focus more than ever before? Could God have wisely allowed what He could have easily prevented, knowing that the enemy's own plans for my destruction were the very ingredients needed to develop the image of me that He had always seen to be true?

It was not an overnight journey, but thankfully, God is the God of Isaiah 30:18: "And therefore the Lord earnestly waits; expecting, looking, and longing to be gracious to you; and therefore He lifts Himself up, that He may have mercy on you and show loving-kindness to you" (AMPC). The truth of God's real nature and the reality of who He sees me to really be has become clearer over time, and yet there is much I have yet to comprehend. It's good that the process itself holds such immense riches, not just the outcome.

The truths that God brought out during that season, through Scripture as well as through the *Monolith* photograph, have stood the test of time and continue to provide rich ground for further exploration:

Our lives are God's masterpiece. The way we are known in heaven is His reality. Who we come from is greater than what we've come through.

God deeply enjoys our process of development, as we perceive more clearly the loving, imaginative Master Creator that He is; drawing out the beautiful image of us that He sees, until we can see it too.

As His image of us continues to emerge in our hearts, our lives become an evidence of His creative genius, unchanging love, and empowering grace.

We are meant to be masterpieces that fully reflect who God really is, while uniquely expressing who He created us to be: a labor of love that people find themselves drawn to and ask:

"Who is this Master Artist? And does He have an image of me like that?"

THE MASTER'S EYES VS. EARTH-BOUND PERSPECTIVES

God imagined our lives before time ever was. He sees us from a heaven-based vantage point that is timeless, elevated, and glorious in Christ. Our journey is not a recent event to Him. The God of eternity is not dashing about, wondering what He's going to do now based on our most recent crisis.

Your story is already written—and God is an excellent writer.

The Amplified Bible, Classic Edition version of Psalm 139:13-17 says:

> For You did form my inward parts; You did knit me together in my mother's womb. I will confess and praise You for You are fearful and wonderful and for the awful wonder of my birth! Wonderful are Your works, and that my inner self knows right well.

> My frame was not hidden from You when I was being formed in secret and intricately and curiously wrought, as if embroidered with various colors in the depths of the earth, a region of mystery.

> Your eyes saw my unformed substance, and in Your book all the days of my life were written before ever they took shape, when as yet there was none of them.

How precious and weighty also are Your thoughts to me, O God!
How vast is the sum of them!

Each of us has a divine and unique identity and destiny that God can clearly see. Our process of development is the journey we embark on with Him until His reality about our lives becomes ours as well.

When we embrace His timelessness, we can let go of perceiving our lives only through the lens of the here and now. We gain the perspective of living in our present based on our promises for the future: "For I know the thoughts and plans that I have for you, says the Lord, thoughts and plans for welfare and peace and not for evil, to give you hope in your final outcome" (Jeremiah 29:11, AMPC).

> **God has already written the story of our lives, so He**
> **is never gripped about the current chapter. However,**
> **He is intent on using every circumstance for our**
> **process of development so that we will grow into the**
> **fullness of our identity in Christ.**

When we understand that every situation we encounter is contributing to our growth, then we exchange circling our circumstances like a dog chasing its tail for a spiral staircase of process that adds elevation to our perspective. If we continue to try to understand our true identity by solving all of our problematic issues, then we end up going round and round at an earth-bound level, expending huge amounts of energy but never rising above our current situation to see it through the eyes of the Father and comprehend it with the mind of Christ.

By understanding that everything in our lives can be an opportunity to become more like the image God already sees us as, we begin to build a progressive spiral stairway of truth that aligns us with His elevated perspective. We may well revisit previous areas of development, but it will always be at a higher and higher place each time. From this viewpoint, God continues to become bigger and our ground-level circumstances continue to get smaller, as we ascend in His peace, joy, and security of His unchanging love.

No matter what our current mess may appear to be, like the back of a beautiful embroidered tapestry, the knots and loose threads are not what God focuses on. He sees the front piece of our lives: the artistic, finished image of who we really are, woven through Christ in us, our hope of glory.

**Timeless, elevated, and glorious. That's how the
Master's eyes see.**

THE VALUE OF THE DARKROOM

Seeing the masterpiece God created us to be is a process of development. Often, the rules we thought should apply have evaporated. Transformation takes longer than we anticipated and everyone else seems to be progressing faster than we are. We long for God to turn on the light and show us what the outcome of our lives will be! We're tempted to settle for a postcard snapshot of our destiny and get on with it. Isn't there a self-help inventory or a program with five easy steps instead?

But no one describes a postcard reproduction as a priceless work of art. God only deals in original masterpieces: "For we are God's masterpiece. He has created us anew in Christ Jesus, so we can do the good things he planned for us long ago" (Ephesians 2:10, NLT). The word "masterpiece" can also be translated as "workmanship"—the work of a greatly skilled craftsman.

In the old days of photography, each image had to be created by hand. Every printing process was different based on the temperature, chemicals, and special requirements of the negative used. In the middle of the process, everything looked like a mess and the image was difficult to discern. But a master photographer never considers those things, because he knows that they are simply the necessary steps to the outcome of the image that he already sees in his mind.

The darkroom times of life are not God trying to be difficult. When we know the true nature of the Father who is in charge of this process, we can be at rest, knowing that He can be trusted. When our circumstances don't make sense or our progress seems to be taking too long, God can be someone for us now that He couldn't be at any other time. It's the perfect place to see a new aspect of His true self that begins to reveal a more accurate image of who we really are, too.

At those times, He smiles as our full weight rests in His hands. In that place of peace, we are allowing Him to "create us anew in Christ." God is not renovating your old man that died but is revealing the new life that already lives in you. "For you died to this world, and your new, real life is hidden with Christ in God" (Colossians 3:3, AMPC).

**Like an image already exposed on photographic
paper, your real life is already hidden with Christ in**

PROLOGUE

**God. It just needs a process of development for us
and others to see it clearly.**

As we encounter and understand how the process of our true identity emerges, "darkroom days" can actually be ones we look forward to. They may be times of deep renewal, where we know that the revelation that God deposits will come into the light in due time. For now, we soak in the majesty of His grace, the assurance of His peace, and the depths of His joy that bring strength until it's time—His time—for the next stage of the image He sees to be revealed.

THE BRIDGE FROM CONCEPT TO REALITY

There's always a gap from concept to reality in any area of our lives. When we initially hear transformational truth, we often respond with joy. But our initial positive reaction is not a guarantee that the seed taking root in our lives will bear mature fruit (Matthew 13:20-21). How many great conferences have we gone to where we have been genuinely touched, but months later we remain unchanged because our breakthrough lacked followthrough? The sessions may have led to a "mountaintop experience," but that is not how God designed us to live. As I wrote about extensively in my first book, *Joyful Intentionality*, transformation is a relational process with God that occurs as we travel and requires our passionate participation.

Identity often has one of the widest chasms of truth between how we see ourselves and how God sees us. There will be things that you thought to be true that are not actually the truth about who God really is and who you really are. Those discoveries leave missing pieces that God delights in filling. There are places where we need to unlearn lessons from our history and exchange them for seeing the life God has always envisioned. These are the occasions that the Holy Spirit looks forward to, because He loves His job as our brilliant Teacher, Helper, and Comforter.

This book is a tool for you to discover the truths that span the gaps in your true identity so that you gain the clear lenses necessary to see the image of yourself that God does. It is a bridge for you to cross that will take you from biblical concepts you may have heard into the living reality of your identity as heaven sees you. Far too often, we've read books that told us what our identity in Christ should be, but we've missed the tangible tools to establish the truth in our daily experience. Either the learning was all conceptual or we were handed a one-dimensional how-to manual. Many times, we know the right answers, but having it become the way we perceive, think, speak, and act remains elusive.

THE MINDSETS OF IDENTITY

In this book, we'll explore how lasting transformation into the image of Christ occurs and the heaven-based lenses to view our lives through. How do people think when they see themselves as God does? And how does that manifest in their everyday life—in their language, choices and actions? What are the common obstacles they face, and how do they partner with the Holy Spirit in overcoming them?

THE GUIDEBOOK

Along with this book, there is a guidebook. Like a travel guide you pick up before a road trip, this is a tool for interpreting the journey of identity, interacting with God about your discoveries, and following through the breakthroughs you encounter as you read *The Image*. There is no lasting breakthrough without followthrough. We must not only take our internal territory, but must establish it so that this book doesn't just become a one-time encounter, but part of your continuing lifestyle, reflected in your perceptions, mindsets, language, and actions, as well as how you see and think about yourself, God, and others.

Read the opening article in the guidebook on how God uses questions. Yes, there are questions for you to explore each chapter, however, they are not quizzes of comprehension. They are relational questions to spark interaction between you and God, as well as any others you might be sharing this experience with. They can be done individually or in groups. You'll find opportunities to have new, more brilliant thoughts and be given practical tools for discovering the clues to who God made you to truly be.

After you've explored those questions, we'll walk through the experience of putting words to your identity and give you some creative ideas for how to use and expand an Identity Statement.

IDENTITY IS A JOURNEY

The concept of my true identity in Christ is something that He's been actively revealing for quite a while, and it's been a journey that has revolutionized my life. In recent years, I've shared these teachings and ideas at identity workshops and conferences around the world, watching countless people become empowered and equipped. We regularly receive emails from people who joined us for these sessions a year or two ago and are still encountering a powerful process of development. For those of us in community together, we continue to watch the amazing evidences of transformation that still leave us in awe as we connect more and more with Christ in us, our true hope of glory.

Identity is a progressive experience with God, not an assignment to be completed. Allow His image of you to develop at a pace of the Holy Spirit's choosing. Embrace the aspects of yourself that are unique to you and revel in the joy that no two true masterpieces are alike. It's impossible to compare a Van Gogh painting to a Rembrandt and say one is better than the other. They are both equally priceless, totally distinct, and absolutely beautiful.

There's no one quite like you. It's a thought that makes God smile.

PART 1

THE IMAGE

INTRODUCTION

THE MAN IN THE MIRROR

But we all, with unveiled face, beholding as in a mirror the glory of the Lord, are being transformed into the same image from glory to glory, just as by the Spirit of the Lord.

2 CORINTHIANS 3:18

How do humans know what they look like? Long ago, people caught their reflection in a pool of water—later, it was on polished stones or smooth pieces of copper. Eventually, we learned how to coat a piece of glass and create a mirror that accurately reflected our appearance.

In 2 Corinthians 3:18, Paul was writing to the local church at Corinth about the differences between the days of the Old Testament law and the times they were in now. Like many early (and some current-day) churches, the truths of God's new covenant nature were being processed through an old-covenant lens. Paul wanted them to see who God was now, not just then, and encourage them that the fading glory of God's goodness that radiated from Moses after being in God's presence was different on this side of the cross (2 Corinthians 3:13). Because Christ is now in us and never leaves us, our comprehension of the glory of who He really is increases from glory to the next level of glory.

In fact, "Christ in you, the hope of glory" (Colossians 1:27) is a mystery that God is continuously revealing to us. We are in the repeated process of accurately seeing Him more clearly. And as God's spirit of wisdom and revelation continues to enlighten the eyes of our hearts in the knowledge of Him (Ephesians 1:18), we see the next level of His true nature. Though, as soon as we begin to understand and encounter it—WHAM—there's another facet of God's goodness . . . or His kindness . . . or . . . no, wait! Look! That's Him as the gracious and faithful One! We gaze at

His glory, only to have it reveal another aspect of His glory—from glory, to glory, to glory. In that living relationship, we need the Spirit of the Lord and the mind of Christ just to keep up with Him!

I find it interesting that 2 Corinthians 3:18 says that we "behold in a mirror the glory of the Lord." Why isn't it looking through a window to see His glory? Or a telescope? Why do we behold His glory in a mirror?

Because when we look in the mirror of God's
glorious goodness, we're meant to see the identity of
Christ in us reflected back.

On this side of the cross, when God looks at us, He sees His Son, Jesus—the perfect reflection of what God imagined when He made man in His image: the Christ who absorbed all of our sin and our fatal flaws and took them as His own. Since the just payment for sin is death, Jesus' body died. His perfect life paid in full the demands of the old law, once and for all. This opened the door for a new law based on liberty and love. Once the law of life in Christ was the new rule book, Jesus was the first to experience it. When sin is paid for, life returns! (James 2:12; Romans 8:2; Ephesians 2:14; 2 Corinthians 5:17; Philippians 2:13; Colossians 1:18, 21.)

In that way, the whole world was reconciled to God, ready to be redeemed when they recognized this great gift and said, "I agree. I can't fix my own life or pay for my own sins and Jesus loved me enough to do it for me. I accept that as the truth."

At that moment, the image of the man in the mirror
is forever changed, from the old man that you were
to the image of the Son of God: "Christ in you, your
hope of glory" (Colossians 1:27).

"For if we have been united together in the likeness of His death, certainly we also shall be in the likeness of His resurrection, knowing this, that our old man was crucified with Him, that the body of sin might be done away with, that we should no longer be slaves of sin. For he who has died has been freed from sin" (Romans 6:5-7).

From this point forward, life for us becomes a continuing process of accurately seeing the image of Christ in us that God already sees. We don't need the lens of a telescope, because God is no longer far away (Ephesians 2:13). We're not looking through a window, because there is no barrier between us (Ephesians 2:14). No longer do we have to stand at a distance, hoping to connect with God. He now lives in us, never leaving or forsaking us (Hebrews 13:5). When we read the New Testament, we're reading our story of the New Man or New Woman we are in Christ. Through the knowledge of who God really is, we are meant to constantly connect more and more with the divine power that has already given us all things that pertain to life and godliness (2 Peter 1:3).

So how does the process of transformation occur until we accurately reflect the image of Christ's identity in us? Is it by working hard to remember and obey all the rules? Or by getting a graduate degree? Or filling in lots of workbooks? It is not.

Transformation is not initiated by doing. It starts with beholding.

Second Corinthians 3:18 says that it is in beholding His glory that we "are being" (progressive tense) transformed into His same image. In our worship, meditation, thanksgiving, and extended times in one passage of Scripture or relational prayer, we keep gazing at and encountering who God really, really is. We look … and look … and look again at His true nature, until our relationship with God is as real to us as ours already is to Him. And we realize that in all that looking, gazing, and encountering, we've become amazingly like Him.

It was true of the disciples. "The members of the council were amazed when they saw the boldness of Peter and John, for they could see that they were ordinary men with no special training in the Scriptures. They also recognized them as men who had been with Jesus" (Acts 4:13, NLT). These men were not only unschooled in the Scriptures, they weren't always the brightest bulbs in the box when it came to practical ministry; but they had undergone a significant, recognizable transformation that even their adversaries conceded. Their image had been altered by their extended time with Jesus and the indwelling of the Holy Spirit. They had seen who God really was and in the process had become an increasingly accurate reflection of Him to the world around them. As He was, so were they becoming in this world (1 John 4:17).

Nothing has changed in 2,000 years. When we look at our lives, there should be a growing resemblance to the true nature of God that is reflected back to us and to everyone we meet.

So how come it doesn't always work like that?

FUN HOUSE MIRRORS

The quality of a mirror impacts the reflection of ourselves that we see. Remember the crazy mirrors in the carnival funhouse? Some gave us long legs and little bodies. Others made us short and wide. As kids, we always spent the most time in that part of the funhouse, stepping closer, backing up—watching how our images changed and laughing at each other and ourselves. While it was amusing to us then, it also made me wonder now: what if the same principle pertains to spirituality?

When we think about the concept of beholding as a
key to transformation, what happens if the image of
Christ in us is being reflected in a "mirror" that is
not accurate?

While Satan is not all-knowing, he's also not completely stupid. Sometimes, he understands the principle of "beholding and becoming" better than we do. He has realized that if he can warp the image of God that you see, you will still become what you behold.

The evidence of this is all around us. We see people who have beheld God as a distant, faraway deity—so they feel hopeless to find Him in their daily lives. Or sadly, they've been taught that obedience is best motivated by fear, so they have become either fearful or someone to be feared. The reality is that obedience is best motivated by love (John 14:15) and that it is God who works in us both to will and to do what He desires most (Philippians 2:13). The Galatians had tinted their mirror with old-covenant laws that no longer applied in a New Testament world. The church at Ephesus had lost sight of their relational love of God, trying-harder-to-do-better for Him instead with all their good works (Revelation 2:1-5).

What you may have heard or learned or
encountered in people regarding the nature of God
doesn't mean that He is really like that.

Our childhood experiences with fathers, whether they were wonderful, absent, or harsh, shape our concept of Father God. Some of us had delightful times at church as small children, but others may have experienced Sunday school as a place where you needed to remember lots of rules, your memory verse and lesson, or there was a sense that God was disappointed because you had failed.

A recent study polled thousands of people in America who described themselves as Christians and found them to have four main views of God:[ii]

- He is engaged in our lives but angry, actively prosecuting us for our sins.
- He is distant and not actively engaged but still mad about the state of things.
- He is not judgmental, but He is also distant and unreachable.
- He is benevolent and kind, fully engaged in our everyday lives.

Only 24 percent of those responding described God as benevolent and engaged, which means that 76 percent of people in that survey are looking into a very warped mirror.

Our starting point in any exploration of our true identity must begin with accurately understanding who we perceive God to be.

The Father, Jesus, and Holy Spirit chose what we would look like when we were created. They wanted us to look like them! "Then God said, 'Let Us make man in Our image, according to Our likeness'" (Genesis 1:26). Humans were given a small piece of territory, a garden, to practice in and learn from with the intent that they would grow into full authority on the earth. A garden implies some degree of cultivation. They weren't being thrown into a vast expanse, but a prepared starting place, in face-to-face relationship with a God who adored them.

Adam and Eve were created as beloved ones of God, clothed in the glory of His goodness, reflecting His image on earth as it was in heaven. God made sure they had the freedom to choose relationship with Him, giving them tremendous permission and stewardship, as well as an opportunity to trust Him with what was beyond their realm of authority at that time. We know that God planned for them to have dominion over the earth (Genesis 1:26), but they didn't have it yet. They had a prepared garden to learn in and a created environment to grow in relationship with Him.

What the Father, Jesus and Holy Spirit had given the first man and woman was precious and powerful—and Satan devised a plan to get them to give it away. It's how con artists work today. They don't wrestle our belongings away from us like a purse snatcher. They cultivate fear and doubt, hoping that you'll give away your credit card or personal information for quick riches or to fix a problem that doesn't exist.

The enemy began with stirring up doubt: "Did God really say . . ." (Genesis 3:1: NLT). He began to warp the image of God's true identity, bending it just enough to imply that God might not be trustworthy or generous; and then hoped that Eve and Adam would try to meet their own needs through their own means, thereby giving away the truth of who God really was and who they were created to be: a man and woman in His likeness for whom He had completely and totally provided.

THE MAN IN THE MIRROR

So who do you see God to be in your life? What experiences may have impacted the way you view Him and may have caused you to wonder if He is really who He says He is? Have you been introduced to an old covenant identity of God where our relationship is based on rules, a New Testament image of grace, or a mixture of both? The answer to these questions are the foundation on which all of your identity will be built, because what we think about God is the bedrock of our spirituality.

> **Our perception of God's true identity impacts our understanding of who He made us to truly be. If our image of Him is not accurate, then our image of ourselves will not be either.**

Second Corinthians 3:18 says, "But we all, with unveiled face, beholding as in a mirror the glory of the Lord, are being transformed into the same image from glory to glory, just as by the Spirit of the Lord." Verse 14 says that "the veil is taken away in Christ." We are no longer trying to catch a glimpse of God through the old covenant of regulations but have been redeemed into a living, face-to-face relationship with the Father, Son, and Holy Spirit. But Satan would love to continue to substitute a warped image of God, shaped by poor histories and experiences, that will stir up doubt as to His identity and ours.

The promise of 2 Corinthians 3:14 is that we can behold a clear, accurate image of God. In Christ, we are meant to encounter His love, joy, peace, kindness, gentleness, patience, and goodness in a way that is transformational in our lives, until "as He is, so are we in this world" (1 John 4:17).

Transformation into our true identity does not occur through trying-harder-to-do-better-for-God or applying logic to understand His ways. It is seeing Him accurately in the Word and encountering His true nature as the One who actually was the Word (John 1:14). The life of Christ in us is our hope of glory, because it is an accurate, true image of who God really is that will reflect who we were created to be. The image we were meant to behold and become is not our own, nor is it of a deity shaped by our poor experiences, religion, doubt, or fear.

It is Jesus—our Man in the Mirror.

YOUR PROVISION HAS BEEN PACKED

So prepare to embark on an adventure with God. Feel the warmth of your hand in the hand of Jesus and the smile of the Holy Spirit as He beams with excitement. The same God who revealed Himself while walking in the garden with His first human friends adores walking with you just as much. It is what we were created for: to be loving friends of a Loving Friend. Jesus was the last Adam, the One who got it right (2 Corinthians 15:22, 45). In Him, we can have the relationship with God that was always intended. Our journey is learning how to live in it, grow in it and discover our identity as He has always imagined us to be.

Every trip requires luggage and the Father has packed yours for you, full of every provision that you will need:

- His joyful expectancy for your good outcome
- Grace that empowers
- Revelation and enlightenment for the eyes of your heart to see clearly
- Love that expands all "impossibles" into possibilities

He will guide you with the compass of His true nature and the kiss of His permission to explore. And while the map of where you travel will be yours to uniquely draw with Him, here are a few of the territories that He will be handing you the keys to in this book:

- Your #1 identity in the Kingdom
- Overcoming our greatest fear
- Discovering opportunities right next to occasions for offense
- Continually updating our image of God and ourselves
- The freedom of knowing your assignments in the Kingdom
- The promises that provision your identity

This is your story and journey with God, not anyone else's. Allow Him to set your pace. Let go of the weights of comparison to anyone else's path because God doesn't use them. Release the baggage of lies, poor thoughts and inaccurate perceptions that spiritual identity thieves have tried to lure you with. Embrace the companionship and provision of the Holy Spirit as your "…Helper (Comforter, Advocate, Intercessor—Counselor, Strengthener, Standby), the Holy Spirit, whom the Father will send in My name…He will teach you all things. And He will help you remember everything that I have told you" (John 14:26, AMPC).

This is the kind of book that will not be finished when you've turned the last page. Your introduction to the process of Kingdom identity will have completed its first exploration, but you will find yourself revisiting the content and questions again and again as you continue to explore the next level of your life in Christ with Him. Transformation does not occur in one-time events that are here today and gone tomorrow. We may have encounters that impact us greatly, but each is meant to release a process of establishing our experiences into a lifestyle with God. It's called "abiding" (John 15:4).

YOU ARE WORTH ENOUGH

A few years ago, I did an identity workshop with a large number of people. The room was packed and we had a dynamic day of exploring together. As our time came to a close, I asked folks to take a piece of paper and jot down one new truth or discovery that they were taking away from the sessions.

After a fabulous dinner with friends, I returned to the home of my hosts and began to prepare for bed. I was still pretty energized from the day, so I decided to spread out all the little papers that I had collected. It's always interesting to see the wide variety of comments on a teaching and workshop experience. There were many people who named key points and were able to repeat very specific aspects of what I had shared. As I continued to read, I felt a growing satisfaction that people were connecting well with the material that I had so carefully prepared.

And then I opened a small scrap of lined yellow paper. It did not contain a long paragraph or quote extensive parts of my well-crafted message. It simply said:

> **"I discovered that I am worth enough to have an identity in God."**

It stopped me cold. No matter how long I stared at the paper, I couldn't quite comprehend the words. There was at least one person in that room who had never felt worthy enough to even have an identity in God—much less explore it. How many others were there? I'm guessing more than one.

My starting point for the exploration of identity forever changed after that day. I keep that little paper in a frame in my office to remind me that this is where all of identity begins. It begins in knowing that you are worth having a unique, beautiful, God-created identity in Christ. Too many people around us don't know that yet. I started out as one of them. You may have too. Family, friends, co-workers—women and men we connect with every day might also be in the very same place. But this brave woman had the courage to say so.

God is delighted that you're sitting here, thinking about His true nature and who He created you to be. He knows exactly who you really are and how this process works, as well as the grace and mercy it will require. He knows and He prepared for it long before you were ever born.

Above all else, you are worth it to Him. You are His beloved one. If you don't know that yet or long to explore that aspect of His nature more fully, then keep reading. It's the first territory that we'll unlock together.

CHAPTER 1

OUR PRIMARY IDENTITY

Awards ceremonies are interesting occasions, and as a former school teacher and wife of a soccer coach, there have been more than I can count. I've been present at numerous Christian conferences where outstanding members were honored, and yet I can't say that I've always paid close attention to the speeches. What intrigues me is watching the responses of the people in the crowd—before, during, and after awards are given. So for this first truth about identity, I'd like you to use your God-given imagination for a moment. Pause . . . be still and at rest . . . and imagine yourself at such a ceremony in a wonderful community that you have been a part of for many years, when a leader that you greatly respect, rises and says:

"I'd like to honor someone amongst us tonight who has been incredibly faithful, joyful in every circumstance, with strong gifts and great boldness of faith. But more important, they are dearly beloved by God, and they radiate His friendship in a way that encourages others continually. They are a champion of the faith and, we believe, destined for true greatness in the Kingdom. They make the Father smile, and He is well-pleased in who they are and are becoming.

"When I call your name, would you kindly come to the front of the room?"

What would happen at that moment for you? Would you be confident that it was your name about to be called? Or would you be certain that it wasn't? What if it was? How would it feel to hear your name?

Would you feel honored or unworthy? Delighted or embarrassed? Relieved or incredibly surprised? Grateful or flustered?

If you can, try to set aside what you think are the spiritually appropriate answers and really consider what it feels like to be identified as the person described here. How does it feel to hear the words "We choose you"?

THE POWER OF BEING CHOSEN

There is something incredibly powerful about being chosen. We feel the thrill of being picked first for a sports team or having the teacher call on our raised hand in class. Maybe we auditioned for a play and got the part. Many of us have labored over résumés for dream jobs, hoping to create a document that will cause us to be selected. Political elections are one of the most expansive (and expensive) processes of choice, where candidates in essence are all saying "Pick me!" And then there is the wonderful experience of having the man or woman you love say, "I choose you."

Of course, the flip side of being chosen is not being chosen—also known as rejection. Instead of hoping to be chosen first in a schoolyard pick, we stand quietly just praying not to be the last one left. We may watch as others in our place of employment are given one opportunity after the next, while all our hard work seems to be forgotten. We struggle to enter the pool of candidates for a leadership position in a ministry because everyone else seems so much more qualified, or have someone we love choose to love someone else.

> **Why are the words "I choose you" so powerful and**
> **affirming? It's because God laid the foundation of**
> **our true identity on them.**

John 15:16 says, "You did not choose Me, but I chose you and appointed you that you should go and bear fruit, and that your fruit should remain . . ."

Second Thessalonians 2:13-14 says, "God from the beginning chose you for salvation through sanctification by the Spirit and belief in the truth, to which He called you by our gospel, for the obtaining of the glory of our Lord Jesus Christ."

There is an inherent sense of worth in being chosen. It is an act that communicates "I see value in you, and I want you to be with me." The verses in 2 Thessalonians indicate that God has not chosen you in a last minute switch because He couldn't find someone better. "From the beginning . . ." places us back into Psalm 139 and all of our days being written long ago. Before you ever had a chance to succeed or fail, God chose you. That's important to understand.

**God did not choose you based on your behavior, so
how can He accept you more or less because of it?**

OUR PRIMARY IDENTITY

Our behavior can impact our fellowship with God, but once we are in Christ, it does not define our identity with Him. God's relationship is with Christ in us. It's not based on performance but our position in Him. Ephesians 1:5-6 says, "Having predestined us to adoption as sons by Jesus Christ to himself, according to the good pleasure of His will, to the praise of the glory of His grace, by which He made us Accepted in the Beloved." And there it is:

**Our primary identity is that we are
Accepted in the Beloved.**

Every aspect of our true identity in Christ rests on this living truth. No matter what our history may have been, no matter how hard it seems to believe some days, being the Accepted in the Beloved is the straight and true mirror in which the image of Christ in us is reflected. God chose you, and you are fully accepted because God fully accepts Jesus. You can't earn what has already been given. Your point of action is to receive it and then abide in it, to look into the mirror of Christ and say, "Yup, that's who I am and am becoming."

Your true identity is based on who Jesus is to the Father. Once we agree and embrace Jesus' true identity in the action that we refer to as salvation, then God always sees us in Christ. Life for us becomes a continuing journey of response to the truth of who He really is and who we really are as the Accepted in the Beloved—until it's as real for us as it has always been to Him.

**Just as God's true identity is always our starting
point, being Accepted in the Beloved is where He
begins with us.**

It is important to note that the weight of establishing this concept as our reality is never on us. Who is initiating the action in all of these verses? God is doing the choosing. He is the one who "made" us accepted and adopted us as His blood-bought, full-fledged children. It's His will and His grace that are in action. Even our love for Him is initiated by Him. "We love Him, because He first loved us" (1 John 4:19).

On the day of your earthly birth, you were given a last name based on the family that you had been born into. You didn't have to pass a test or demonstrate basic skills to be given that name. When you behaved poorly, no one took your last name away. There may have been consequences for your actions, but it did not change who you are known as. In Christ, we were birthed into a new life and a new identity. When we were born again, our family name became "Accepted in the Beloved." Being Accepted in the Beloved is not something you achieve; it's who you are. It's as if God issued you a New Birth Certificate and this is now the name He knows you by. Our journey is to receive and respond to our first and true identity in Christ, learning how to live and thrive in it.

JESUS LOVES ME?

So why do so many men and women seem to struggle to believe this basic truth? Why does living with a profound sense of being Accepted in the Beloved remain more of a concept than a reality for a large number of people?

For years, I knew all the right answers to the question "Does God love me?" After all, it was one of the first songs that I learned as a child—"Jesus loves me, this I know . . ." except that this concept for me looked more like a funhouse mirror of who Father God really was. As with many of us, there were enough unfortunate experiences in my childhood for Satan to point to as false evidence of what acceptance and love actually were, relying heavily on his original question found in Genesis 3:1 again and again: "Has God really said . . .?" "Is God really who He claims be, and can His love and grace truly be that amazing?"

Our adversary in this life is a father too: a father of lies (John 8:44) who seeks to reproduce you in his warped image. Think about it. Satan has never once told you the truth. He is incapable of it. He cannot create or bring life. He can only steal, kill, and destroy it (John 10:10). When you think about each of these actions, they are a reaction to what already exists. To have something stolen, it must already be in your possession. Life must be present before it can be killed. You can't destroy something that hasn't already been created.

Jesus not only came with life but came with it in abundance. He *is* the creator, the original author of our story, and the giver of good gifts (Hebrews 12:2 and Ephesians 4:8). The riches of relationship, our life in the Beloved, and what He is building in you were presented to you fully on the day of your new birth. It is your family inheritance. You may not have come into all of it yet, but He has (past tense) given us all things that pertain to life and godliness (2 Peter 1:3).

It's yours, so our enemy's only hope is that you never fully receive it. And if you do begin to realize who you are as the Accepted in the Beloved, he works to steal, kill, or destroy that truth before it becomes as real to us as it is to God.

"NOTHING IN THAT BAG FOR ME"

I first realized that such an identity theft had occurred in my own life while watching my favorite movie: *The Wizard of Oz*. This film was an icon in my household. I knew all the songs practically before I could talk, since my mother apparently used to sing them to me before I was born. For me, Santa did not employ elves. Couldn't everyone see that they were obviously munchkins? I was fascinated by the tornado, cheered for Toto when he escaped Miss Gulch, and could skip to school just like Dorothy did down the Yellow Brick Road.

But I enjoyed the movie most after it became available on videotape, because then I could fast forward over the one part for which I always, *always* left the room when I was a child. It was the scene following the triumphant return of Dorothy and her pals to receive their reward from the Wizard for killing the Wicked Witch. The Scarecrow got his diploma. The Tin Man got his heart. The Lion got his medal for courage.

Yet when the Wizard came to Dorothy, he awkwardly paused. I can still hear her voice and see her eyes as she said, "I don't think there's anything in that bag for me." I always wanted the Wizard to say, "Of course there is!"—but he never did. He looked sad too, as if to agree that while he might have enough for the others, he had simply run out by the time he got to Dorothy. Her challenges were too great to overcome.

I was in my early 30s when I pulled out my favorite recording and curled up to watch my pals as their story unfolded . . . again. And as usual, when the Wizard got out his black bag, I hit the fast forward button.

"Why do you always do that?" a voice resonated inside of me. I stopped for a moment. I had never really given it much thought, other than it always made me sad. The Holy Spirit kindly asked again, "Why don't you ever want to watch that part of the movie?" I realized that I didn't really know. So, I intuitively did what I've since learned to do when God is asking questions: I asked Him to tell me the answer. (I won't mention here how long it's taken me to learn this on a consistent basis. Let's just say, probably longer than it will take you.)

What I remember most was His tone. It was deeply affectionate, incredibly gentle, and full of understanding for what I had yet to comprehend.

"Because . . . you think I'm like that too."

I knew in an instant that it was true. Based on my experiences, God was like the Wizard: not as big as He first appeared to be and limited in what He could really do. But most of all, life was about standing in line while everyone else appeared to receive wonderful things from Him, only to run out just when it seemed to be my turn.

Then, He continued, whispering with a smile, "It's a lie. So let's not believe it anymore."

Let's . . . Let us . . . Let US not believe it anymore. I remember the impact of those words. It was one of my earliest encounters with the partnership of the Holy Spirit. Of course, He didn't believe the lie, but His language told me that He would be my Steadfast Helper, my Comforter and partner in sorting out the truth.

It was the beginning of understanding the concept of "unlearning," though it would be years before I had the language to go with my encounter. I had believed something about God that was not true, and it had distorted how I perceived my value to Him. Over the next few years, God and I had lots of these conversations, and I discovered that His way of bringing us into alignment with His truth was rarely about exploring the lie in depth. He comes in with truth and light that illuminate with revelation. We recognize what it is together, and I have the joy of choosing to no longer believe the lie, no matter what circumstances or history try to validate it. I get to focus, fill up on and embrace whatever God's truth is instead. When it's time to unlearn a lie, it's an occasion to ask two of the best questions of all:

**"Father, what is the opposite in Your true nature to
this lie?" and "What's Your truth about my identity
because of this?"**

"Unlearning" occurs through recognition of the untruth, but it is rejoicing, thanksgiving and thinking deeply about the truth found in God's Word that displace it. In my *Wizard of Oz* encounter, I had recognized that I was willing to accept the benevolent nature of God for others, but the truth of "Jesus loves me" had been substituted for a lie based on poor experiences. It was time to immerse myself in Scripture, teaching, meditation, and divine conversation (also known as prayer) about just how beloved and chosen Allison was—not just Allison's friends.

It would be a process, a spiral staircase, that would be built in the coming years, but I continued to encounter the tenacious kindness of God coming face to face and saying, "YOU . . . It's you, sweetheart. I chose you. And there will always be exactly what you need in My 'bag' for you. I'm not like the Wizard or other people in your history. This is what I am really, really like."

Life since then has been a relentless march through the territory of His goodness, faithfulness, kindness, mercy—the list goes on and on. Sometimes it is a choice to put faith over feelings. No matter what is occurring or how great my own gaps are, God will always answer the question of who He wants to be for me now. And in the process, I know that I will see more of His true identity and mine.

CHOSEN ONES HAVE ISSUES

Being accepted and chosen isn't about perfection. In fact, God is very specific in who He chooses: He chooses people with issues. Often, we've become so used to the stories of our Bible heroes, we miss the impact of who God has a history of partnering with. Abraham told the local king that his wife Sarah, was his sister to avoid disfavor, a move that put Sarah in danger of ending up as someone else's wife (Genesis 20:2). Moses' passion for justice was admirable, except for the part where it made him so angry he killed a man (Exodus 2:12). This list goes on and on: David slept with his friend's wife and then arranged for an "accident" that killed his friend to cover it up; Elijah was Mr. Super Prophet at Mt. Carmel and yet ran in terror almost immediately, intimidated by Jezebel. These are not small things. And let's not forget the disciples who were arguing about status and title, while walking only a few feet away from Jesus (Mark 9:34), and Paul who didn't just lack the basic qualifications of an apostle but had devoted his life to killing them prior to his conversion!

If you write out these behaviors with contemporary names and create a setting in your local church or community—would you ever think of describing any of these men as:

- "The friend of God"
- "The one who God talked face to face with as a man would with His friend"
- "A man after God's own heart"
- "The one whom Jesus loved"
- "According to the grace of God, a wise master builder"

That's Abraham, Moses, David, John and Paul—all men with problems who were chosen and loved by God.

"Because the foolishness of God is wiser than men, and the weakness of God is stronger than men" (1 Corinthians 1:25); and "But the natural man does not receive the things of the Spirit of God, for they are foolishness to him; nor can he know them, because they are spiritually discerned" (1 Corinthians 2:14).

Lose the weights of trying-harder-to-do-better for God's acceptance or to win His approval. Your qualification is based on being Accepted in the Beloved—Christ in you, your hope of glory; connecting in relationship with the One who loves you best because of whose you are. God accepts us in Christ. We respond to that acceptance.

When He says, "I choose you," we say, "Okay," and then behave in a manner that beautifully reflects our primary identity as beloved ones of a wonderfully holy God.

THE PRIVILEGES OF FAMILY

There's a reason God describes His relationship with us primarily in terms of a family, not a team or a pack. He chose to describe His role in our lives with words like "Father," "Son," and a "friend who sticks closer than a brother" (Proverbs 18:24); and He chose to speak of us as His "children," "brothers, and sisters," "sons and daughters of the Most High God." The God of the universe isn't looking for mere followers, He is looking for a family.

Second Corinthians 6:18 says, "I will be a Father to you, and you shall be My sons and daughters, says the Lord Almighty." In John 15:9, Jesus tells us, "As the Father loved Me, I also have loved you; abide in My love." That love is yours! We don't have to earn it; we just have to remain in it. Zephaniah 3:17 celebrates that "The Lord your God in your midst, The Mighty One, will save; He will rejoice over you with gladness, He will quiet you with His love, He will rejoice over you with singing."

When we live as new creations from our true identity
as someone who is Accepted in the Beloved, then we
live in the freedom of knowing that we are always
welcome, always loved, always rejoiced over.

The enemy is desperate for you to believe that you must earn what God has freely given. It is his way of committing identity theft. Acceptance in the Beloved is the Father's gift. Abiding in it is our response and our joyful responsibility in partnership with the Holy Spirit, our Helper, Teacher and Comforter. Righteousness, holiness, and growing up into all things in Christ are our reasonable service that we're glad to give. Obedience is motivated by love (John 14:15) because we've been so wonderfully loved by God.

Just as each of Jesus' first disciples did, we need to choose whether we will respond to His invitation to follow Him once He has chosen us. It's a free-will decision that we will make continually throughout our lives, not just initially at salvation. God has said, "I choose you, and this is who you really are to Me." Under the duress of circumstances or in the face of our own lack, we have the opportunity to continue to make this choice: to believe He meant what He said and respond by following Him once again through whatever challenges are before us.

When being Accepted in the Beloved is still a concept to us, we're tossed about by the winds of uncertainty, inadequacy and self-doubt. Those are times that we can practice responding to the truth, not just what seems to be true about ourselves and our circumstances. Those times don't have to be times of failure if they become opportunities to be as kind to ourselves in this process as God is with us. It's often through these encounters that the concept of our identity begins to become our reality.

"Let us therefore come boldly to the throne of grace, that we may obtain mercy and find grace to help in time of need" (Hebrews 4:16).

"Or do you think lightly of the riches of His kindness and tolerance and patience, not knowing that the kindness of God leads you to repentance?" (Romans 2:4 NASB).

"Boldness" occurs when we come to His throne of grace in time of need, willing to accept the level of goodness God has toward us. And one of the most transforming ways to encounter it is when we haven't been good—and we discover that it hasn't changed His level of goodness toward us! Kindness melts away our rebellion to live in our own strength. As the Accepted Ones, we realize that we really can climb up, sit on His lap or shoulders, and look out over our lives from His perspective, discover our missing pieces, and receive them from His generous supply of promises, provision, and love.

I recently saw a living example of this in a crafted declaration from one of our recently hired administrators. She was a newer member of our community and, therefore, could have been easily overwhelmed by feeling unfamiliar with the team—not to mention having a toddler, a new baby coming, and another job!

But instead, she chose to articulate who she wanted to be in this pioneering opportunity. It was a fabulous example of God-filled boldness that anticipated potential challenges and was making a predetermined choice to stand in her identity and His. Notice that her declaration is not just an "I" statement but also "we," reflecting her partnership and joyful dependency on the Lord.

As I worship through my administrative tasks, I will produce excellent and creative solutions. My work sessions will consist of potent production and be full of life.

We stand together against a poverty spirit of time and joyfully remember that a day can be filled with a thousand years.

We unlock the wealth of time at my fingertips and praise You for a healthy work/balance life.

There will be beautifully precise communications within the team, and I will be confident in my questions because I am a joy to converse with.

You will help me fully understand the needs of my job and give me the insight to anticipate future needs as we continue to grow.

Lord, thank You that You have specifically placed me as the Member Services Administrator. I belong here.

Now that's knowing your primary identity as the Accepted in the Beloved! It's a wonderful, tangible example of making a predetermined choice to see and think about yourself the way that God does. When pressure comes and doubts begin to rise, this is a tremendous foundation to return to and say, "Hang on a minute! *This* is who God has promised to be for me and through me."

As we continue on this exploration of our truest identity, you'll discover a great many things about who God created you to really be. But the beginning of any statement of identity should be your unique variation of the foundation upon which everything else will be built:

I am chosen by God. I am accepted in the Beloved.
I belong here.

When that truth becomes your primary identity with God, there will be incredible gratitude but no great surprise when the Father rises at the end of the age, takes your hand, and says, "It is My pure delight to honor someone amongst us who has been faithful, as I have been faithful; found joy in every circumstance; a champion who took bold steps of faith because they trusted in who I *Am*; a lover of wisdom and of Me. Allow me to introduce My child, My friend, My dearly beloved, in whom I am well pleased."

Chapter 2

Overcoming Our Deepest Fear

Our deepest fear is not that we are inadequate. Our deepest fear is that we are powerful beyond measure. It is our light, not our darkness, that most frightens us.

We ask ourselves, Who am I to be brilliant, gorgeous, talented, fabulous? Actually, who are you not to be? You are a child of God.

Your playing small does not serve the world. There is nothing enlightened about shrinking so that other people won't feel insecure around you.

*We are all meant to shine, as children do.
We were born to make manifest the glory of God that is within us...*

...And as we let our own light shine, we unconsciously give other people permission to do the same. As we are liberated from our own fear, our presence automatically liberates others.[iii]

I first encountered this passage hanging in a frame on an office wall just as I was opening the door to leave. It noted in small print that it had been taken from Nelson Mandela's Inaugural Speech. Though I had been in and out of that room many times, I had never noticed it before. Maybe it was because, on that particular day, I needed to see it.

I had just left a proposal full of fresh ideas and possibilities, all much greater than what seemed reasonable in the natural, on the empty desk inside. It's one of the inherent risks of being a professional dreamer, explorer, and divine strategist, especially after extended times of meditation on the majesty of God. I tend to become immersed in how amazingly big He really is and before you know it, visionary possibilities begin to bubble up, all of which seem quite reasonable at the time.

But invariably as words are put to paper and those papers are left for someone else to review, a battle can begin in our thinking. Whenever we reveal our dreams for others to see, an internal giant of doubt can start to rise up. He wields the age-old question of identity that seeks to eliminate us from taking the very territory that we were just seeing so clearly:

Who do you think you are?

There are many variations of this question that have been used, but the essence of the inquiry remains the same. David's brothers asked it as he wondered aloud about taking on Goliath. Nehemiah's enemies used it regularly as he inspired Israel to rebuild their ruined walls and fight an enemy who seemed to have the upper hand. The Pharisees assaulted Jesus with it time and time again.

> **But far more likely than a weapon in the hands of an adversary, "Who do you think you are?" is a self-inflicted wound. The first person to doubt our identity is usually us.**

Moses said it at the burning bush (Exodus 3:11). Gideon had his own version, citing his poor family line as proof (Judges 6:15). Joshua needed to be told numerous times by Moses, by God and eventually by his own people, to only be strong and very courageous (Deuteronomy 31:7; Joshua 1:17; 18). Uncle Mordecai's words gave Esther her answer to this question by asking her another: "Yet who knows whether you have come to the kingdom for such a time as this?" (Esther 4:14). This young girl was a very unlikely hero, but an entire nation's fate rested in her ability to trust God and shine brightly.

Negativity is one of the chief assassins of identity, and it must be resisted at all costs when we talk about ourselves or about others. God only speaks to who He sees us as, calling us up higher, not calling us out on what we lack. The exchange with Gideon is a classic for this in Judges 6. God never addresses any of Gideon's excuses—and there are a significant number of them to choose from. He relentlessly speaks only to who Gideon really is: A mighty man of valor. A man who the Lord is with. A victorious man sent by God to save Israel for their enemy. There is absolutely no discussion about the fact that Gideon is not currently displaying any of these character traits.

Does this mean that we can't discuss the gaps we discover in ourselves or others in our process of spiritual maturity? No, we can—because there's a huge difference between heaping negativity and condemnation on a person (or ourselves) and a conversation of assessment without judgment. We need to assess situations and the people in them, but we want to do it from a stance that does not pass judgment in the process. Judgment says that you are bad because you behaved badly. Assessment uses the same questions with others that God uses with us. "What is that person believing about themselves and about God that would cause them to behave like that?" "Who does God see them becoming? Who does He want to be for them in that process?" and "How am I meant to contribute to that process?" As we say often at Brilliant, we want to call people up into their potential, not out on their behavior.

Actions may indeed have natural consequences that will occur, and if the people involved are emotionally unstable or unsafe, personal welfare in all of its forms is paramount and must *always* be given the highest priority. But whenever possible, we want to work with people in terms of their identity, not merely their behavior. The poor choices of today do not have to permanently define the potential of tomorrow. Stepping above the emotions of circumstance, we want to partner with God in seeing the image of ourselves and others that He sees, and speak to that.

THE ESSENCE OF GREATNESS

Shining brightly is not reserved only for legendary figures of history. It is the essence of Christ in us, our hope of glory, offering the world a taste of the Kingdom that Jesus referred to over 80 times in the Gospels. Every follower of Jesus has the capacity to connect on earth with the realities of heaven—a place where people encounter forgiveness, kindness, healing, wisdom, and miracles that transcend natural law or understanding.

> **Being radiant in Christ isn't about us making**
> **ourselves big, but about magnifying a majestic God**
> **to be as big as He really is and then being an accurate**
> **reflection of His true nature.**

It is about courageously believing the outrageous nature of the Gospels: that we are called, chosen, and Accepted in the Beloved to be the ones who turn the world upside down (or right side up as the case may be). It's actually embracing the reality that "as He is, so are we in this world" (1 John 4:17). Each of us has a handcrafted destiny that is founded on us living in the abundance of our true identity in Christ. And, as we've said, living in our true identity is based on seeing the full majesty of the God we are meant to reflect as His representatives on the earth. "Now then, we are ambassadors for Christ, as though God were pleading through us: we implore you on Christ's behalf, be reconciled to God" (2 Corinthians 5:20).

An ambassador travels with the full privileges of his or her country, even though they don't currently reside there. Their embassy is actually considered part of their homeland no matter where it is located. What would life be like at our work places, in our neighborhoods, and in our communities if everywhere we went, people were encountering the Kingdom of God, of which we are full-time residents who just happen to be living on earth for now? A people without fear of God's greatness being manifest anywhere, any place, any time, under any circumstance—and yet doing so in a way that was totally normal. God isn't looking for a supernatural people as much as He is looking for a people who will naturally reflect the fullness of His true nature; and His true nature is to comfort, heal, strengthen, and when necessary, to overcome the physical laws of earth with a greater Kingdom reality.

Greatness is not about wealth, numbers, or notoriety. Shining in our full identity as a child of God has nothing to do with a public stage or having a well-known name. It is found in how accurate a likeness we are of His great nature, whether we are being kind to someone in a grocery store or speaking to a thousand people. As I've been fortunate to be taught, true humility is not only knowing who you are without God, but being just as confident in who you are with Him.

This is evident in many places in Scripture, but David's words in 2 Samuel 22:29-37 are perhaps my favorite.

> For You are my lamp, O Lord; the Lord shall enlighten my darkness.

> For by You I can run against a troop; by my God I can leap over a wall.

> As for God, His way is perfect; the word of the Lord is proven;

> He is a shield to all who trust in Him. For who is God, except the Lord?

> And who is a rock, except our God? God is my strength and power,

> And He makes my way perfect.

> He makes my feet like the feet of deer, and sets me on my high places.

> He teaches my hands to make war, so that my arms can bend a bow of bronze.

> You have also given me the shield of Your salvation;

Your gentleness has made me great.

You enlarged my path under me; so my feet did not slip.

I think we may read this and only see the Lord's part in it. But in every aspect that God manifested His majesty, David had to respond. Yes, the Lord taught David's hands to war, but he still had to actually go and run against a troop, leap over a wall, and fight the battle. God had indeed made the ancient king's path true and straight, but David had to not only walk forward but choose to remain on it. And he had the wisdom to understand that it was the power of God's gentleness that was the foundation of his significance.

**David fully embraced his greatness because he fully
knew how great the Author of it was.**

PERMISSION TO SHINE

Scripture instructs us to "shine as lights in the world" (Philippians 2:15), to be a lamp to people's paths with His truth that has illuminated our lives. At times we are a spotlight that draws people together, or a focused laser that cuts through an obstacle to bring breakthrough. The Christ in us is not just our personal hope of glory, but for everyone we encounter. "You are the light of the world. A city that is set on a hill cannot be hidden. Nor do they light a lamp and put it under a basket, but on a lampstand, and it gives light to all who are in the house. Let your light so shine before men, that they may see your good works and glorify your Father in heaven" (Matthew 5:14-16).

**You were made to be seen. And when you are
reflecting an accurate image of who God really is,
people after His own heart will glorify Him, not you.**

It's true that folks may focus on us as we manifest the greatness of God; therefore, we've tried to play small because of a poor definition of humility. "All of God and none of me" sounds pious, but it's not accurate. *All* of us partnering with *all* of God is how He designed life to be when He chose us. I've always loved the thought I heard shared long ago by one of my favorite teachers, Bob Mumford, on this matter. He said he would collect people's compliments graciously throughout a day of ministry because he realized they were giving him a gift, and gifts should be appreciated. He imagined each compliment as an individual rose; and then before he went to sleep, he would gather them together and present a beautiful bouquet to Jesus with an expression of his deep gratefulness for what they had seen and done together.

Because human beings are prone to wanting a touchable deity (remember the Golden Calf incident in Exodus 32), it is true that some will attach their faith, trust, and confidence to notable people. While God has inspired the man or woman, it's often the impact and familiarity of the messenger that they sincerely develop a great affection for because they are sincerely grateful. Maturity is evidenced when we listen for the common sound of Christ in the messengers we hear. Our ears are tuned to the resonant tone of the fruit of the Spirit—relational words that accurately reflect the love, joy, peace, gentleness, encouragement, empowerment, wisdom, and kindness that is God's true nature, no matter who delivers it.

People who authentically shine have perfected the art of rejoicing in the nature of God as they allow Him to radiate in the unique gifts He's given them, and then seamlessly move out of the way to engage you with Him directly. True ambassadors of the Kingdom understand that while you may want them, who you *need* is Jesus. Wise leaders know that their well-timed absence often herds your dependency in the right direction to the genuine Comforter, Helper, Teacher, and Friend. And the wisdom of knowing this rhythm with God allows Him to entrust them with even more of His brilliance.

SHINING BRILLIANTLY CHALLENGES DIM PLACES

Excellence challenges mediocrity. People who are comfortable with the way things are may be challenged when you choose to pursue the fullness of God. Even though your growth is not meant to highlight their lack of development—it can; and not everyone is gracious about that or even realizes that it is happening. No worries. It's really just another opportunity for us to extend grace, mercy, and patience because most of us have failed that test at some point in our lives and have needed that same grace and mercy for ourselves.

Far too often, a poor definition of humility has prompted people to take those who authentically shine brightly down a peg or two (or three . . . or five), with the idea that it somehow protects everyone. I've always been surprised by the jealousy that exists in ministry, as if your shining brightly could dim my light in any way. My perspective is that we need all the Kingdom wattage we can get! Far too often, the embedded message is, "Be bright, just not too bright, so that the rest of us don't look bad. After all, remember that you're only human."

But Jesus didn't do that. Being "the Light of the World" was one of His chief identities (John 8:12). He's well aware that it is imperfect people who are carrying the Light, and it does not seem to bother Him. In fact, He uses it to full advantage. "But we have this treasure in earthen vessels, that the excellence of the power may be of God and not of us" (2 Corinthians 4:7). The very weakness that we often feel prevents us from being as impactful as God created us to be, is the very thing He adores using for the world to know that it's Him who's at work!

The world is supposed to look at you and say, "Really? That must be God!" And we get to marvel right along with them, not by making apologies for our lack, but by celebrating our partnership with amazing grace. We have His permission to shine, cracks and all, with the glory of God that grows through our continued life of worship, adoration, joyful dependency, and divine relationship with the God who adores us.

**When it comes to light, Jesus' only warning was
about hiding it under a basket (Matthew 5:15).**

THE ELEVATED PERSPECTIVE OF HUMOR

The areas of our "unlikeliness" should be a constant source of amusement to us. It certainly is to God. He thinks it's hilarious to continually gain territory against the enemy in partnership with people who are "cracked pots"—this brilliant, glorious mob of Kingdom pioneers who are still growing up into fully mature sons and daughters. The Father is not panicked, no matter how unlikely we seem. He is that confident in His Son and the genius of the Holy Spirit to make all things possible—even us.

"For you see your calling, brethren, that not many wise according to the flesh, not many mighty, not many noble, are called. But God has chosen the foolish things of the world to put to shame the wise, and God has chosen the weak things of the world to put to shame the things which are mighty" (1 Corinthians 1:26-27). When I read this, I hear "Hey, guys! It's pretty obvious that when we consider your calling compared to what we see in the natural, God is not choosing you based on your appearance, credentials, blood line or IQ." The original disciples in the Gospels were a prototype of who God planned on working through in the New Covenant. They were not the best and the brightest in the beginning, but they were the friends of Jesus. God worked from their potential, not their actual.

Why does God do it like that? "Because the foolishness of God is wiser than men, and the weakness of God is stronger than men" (verse 25). The very least of God's nature is vastly beyond the very best that man has to offer. From His perspective, while we are dearly loved, everything people do, or think, or achieve is "weakness" compared to His majesty. We have a sliding scale of weakness that God doesn't have. It's all short of His true nature (Isaiah 64:6 and Romans 3:23), so why put human categories of "better" or "worse" on it? Our weakness is what Christ in us covers and what the Holy Spirit continually shines through.

> **The reality is that God isn't interested in presenting Himself to suit man's definition of greatness, so He finds Himself under no pressure to choose people who fit that definition either.**

Wouldn't it be revolutionary if we had fun with that truth?

Laughter is acid to Satan. Nothing infuriates him more than when we've been incredibly dense or stupid and we choose to embrace our earthen vessel-ness with joy! "Yup, that would be me, the Beloved One who has a few more things to understand about the mind of Christ!" We're not taking our sin lightly; we adore the gift of repentance, but we also come boldly to the throne of grace, confident in the mercy available in our time of need (Hebrews 4:16). It is an act of faith to not put the weight of human-based perfection on ourselves. We choose to shine out in the world, following Him wherever He leads, learning our lessons, embracing everything as training, taking our best shot whenever possible.

Yes, if we take risks, there will be times that we miss the target. If honest mistakes are made, take responsibility and clean them up—but refuse to cower in smallness, surrendering to fear. Abandon protecting a public reputation that God cares nothing about. We often learn as much from our failures as from our successes. Love the learning. Discover what's missing in your relationship with God that left you vulnerable. Ask Him confidently for it, because it's His good pleasure to give it! Those conversations are never something to dread but to be grateful for.

We accelerate our growth when we practice our learning. Some days, we marvel at the strength of what God has developed in us—and on other days, our failures let us know there is more development needed. It is Jesus' full-time job to intercede for us, to stand in our gaps, praying as we convert our learning into our lifestyle. He already knows where all our missing pieces are, so He's never disappointed. He's too busy working with the Holy Spirit to empower your next process of maturity.

GOD'S GREAT NAME

Consider Joshua's response after the defeat at Ai in Joshua chapter 7. We find Josh wailing to God about why He even brought them across the Jordan at all. "Was it just to have the fun of destroying us?" he moans. (Apparently, the miraculous parting of the Jordan river and the collapse of Jericho's walls had become a dim memory—a common side effect of defeat.) "Oh, that we had been content, and dwelt on the other side of the Jordan!" (Also a frequent mindset of failure: reduce your dream back down to manageable proportions.) "What will I say when Israel turns its back on its enemies?" (Now, we're getting a little closer to what's really going on here.) Then [wait for it ... here it comes ...] "What will You do for Your great name?" Nice try, Josh.

> **But this isn't about you being devastated for the**
> **Lord's great name. It's about being embarrassed over**
> **the loss of yours.**

I adore the Lord's response. There will be no pity parties here thinly veiled as concern for God's reputation. "Get up, Josh" the Father says, probably with a bit of an affectionate sigh. "Why are you on the ground? Israel has sinned." Practical. Pragmatic. Priceless. It makes me smile every time. Here's Josh, tearing up his clothes, rolling about and sobbing after getting his butt kicked in battle, instead of asking God why it happened. The pressure of his circumstances have completely skewed his perception of God's true nature, as if God would actually have brought them all this way just to destroy them for sport. The unexpected defeat creates personal panic and Joshua immediately wants to retreat to a smaller vision outside of his land of promises—the one that doesn't require all this risk, faith, and obedience stuff. Why? Because he is acutely embarrassed in front of the army and nation that he is supposed to be leading.

When we've aimed high and missed, when we were so certain we had heard God, and when for all the best reasons we've charged forward and had our "assets" handed to us on a platter, the last thing we usually feel like doing is having an honest conversation with God. Like dear Josh, we wonder why we ever went for it in the first place. What were we thinking? Maybe God doesn't really care about us after all? Under duress, we quickly dim our light, reducing ourselves and our dreams to something far more reasonable so that we can somehow duct tape the tattered remains of our good name . . . oh . . . and of course . . . God's too (we quickly remember to add).

Let me pause for a moment to be clear. I'm not talking about the people who truly misrepresent who God really is, doing malicious public and private things in the name of the Lord that have absolutely nothing to do with His nature or His desires on the earth. I'm talking about honestly taking risks, stepping out of our boats of logic to pray for the sick, sharing a word of prophetic encouragement, or doing what we genuinely feel the Lord is asking of us. That is what Joshua was doing. He had the Lord's permission to take Ai and His battle plan to do so; it's just that someone disobeyed orders and left the army vulnerable. Had Joshua stopped to ask the Lord why they had been defeated, he might have saved himself a lot of unnecessary emotional trauma—not to mention a perfectly good set of clothes.

And while this is not Joshua's finest moment, he remains one of my most beloved friends in Scripture. The fact that he reacts to the defeat at Ai in this manner has always encouraged me. Like Joshua, even the best of us who love God dearly and have trained under great mentors can be susceptible to reducing our vision when we've gone for greatness and suffered defeat. I have done my fair share of rolling about before the Lord, complete with wailing and wondering why everyone else seems to have normal lives. Joshua has been my go-to guy since I was eight years old, so I'm always heartened that someone who would choose to live in the Tabernacle or climb the mountain with Moses could have his rough days, too.

It's not about avoiding these moments in life. It is about "only being strong and very courageous" in those times, knowing that the Lord, our very personal God, is with us wherever we go.

THE WORLD DOESN'T NEED SMALL PEOPLE

Big problems mean big possibilities; and big possibilities require people who cannot merely think outside the box, but who realize that there actually is no box. They embrace every situation as training to step into the massive opportunities that crisis offers. Failure, unfortunate outcomes, and poor experiences will try to push us back into small, confined zones of risk-free safety. We can't let them.

What would have happened to the future of Israel and the nation of Egypt if Joseph had chosen to play small? He had some excellent reasons to do so. After all, he had been despised for his gifts and the favor he had within his own family, stirring up so much resentment that his brothers sold him into slavery. No doubt, many of us have acted immaturely or prematurely with our revelations, and lots of us have disagreed with our siblings. But how many of us really *were* sold to the passing gypsies because of it? Joseph was.

And just as he is beginning to experience favor with his master Potifar, he's unjustly accused and ends up in prison. Whatever fragile sense of worth that he may have gained could have disappeared forever. He is worse off than he's ever been.

Wouldn't that have been the perfect time to back off, sit in his cell, and stop hoping for any kind of meaningful life? We do not know what Joseph's internal journey was, but we know it was not easy. Psalm 105:19 says, "Until the time that his [Joseph's] word came to pass, the word of the Lord tested him." Satan will use past promises, dreams, and prophecies to mock us and stir up doubt. "Has God really said . . .?" It's as old as the Garden of Eden. "Why not just give up?" our adversary whispers. "Or at best, just sit tight, stay small, don't risk. No one's going to blame you for playing it safe after all you've been through."

> **Meanwhile, God uses those same occasions to refine,**
> **strengthen and train us so that when our manifest**
> **destiny appears, our true identity will be strong**
> **enough to fulfill it.**

The New International Version of Psalm 105:19 says, "till the word of the Lord proved him true." When the day came for Joseph to face the brothers who had sold him into slavery, there was no bitterness left, no perceptions warped by vengeance. "But as for you, you meant evil against me; but God meant it for good, in order to bring it about as it is this day, to save many people alive" (Genesis 50:20).

> **Joseph's journey with God had refined how he**
> **perceived, thought, and spoke about his experience.**
> **He saw his identity and his destiny as the Father**
> **always had.**

God knows the beginning from the end. He saw the outcome of Joseph's life and gave him a look at it in a dream, mostly because He knew that what was ahead would be tough to survive without hope and promises. The Lord understood that what Joseph would encounter would scream at him to stay small just at the time He needed him to be big. And on the day Pharaoh's butler remembered the foreigner who had interpreted his dream in prison, Joseph was ready. God had not authored Joseph's trials, but He partnered with him in overcoming them. This former slave and prisoner was now in a position of leadership and influence over a nation.

Our preparation for our God-given destiny will rarely unfold as we expect, but by using every circumstance as a training ground, we will continue to expand our understanding of who God is for us and who He created us to be. We can allow His promises to become bigger than our adversity or failures—continually expanding our inner territory. The world desperately needs *big*, powerful, joyful, brilliant believers in Jesus Christ who understand their identity as overcomers in this life.

It will take a courageous people of God, who seriously know and are fully persuaded of His true nature and their authentic identity in Christ, who are willing to be as big in this life as God needs us to be. When that happens, our encounters with God as perfect love will have transformed our greatest fear into the world's best hope.

CHAPTER 3
DOORS OF OPPORTUNITY OR OFFENSE

Have you ever noticed how the same event can happen to several different people, and each of them has a unique response? What one person finds overwhelming, another takes in stride. What I might consider a learning experience could be seen as an absolute failure by someone else.

Our identity gives us the lens for how we perceive our lives—both positively and negatively.

It's a key part of having the "eyes to see and ears to hear" that Jesus spoke of so many times in the Gospels.

Elisha gives us a great example of this in 2 Kings 6:17 when he asked God to open the eyes of his servant so that he could share the prophet's reality. These two men were in the same situation but had two very different experiences. Jesus was at complete rest in the storm of Mark 4, while the disciples were certain they were dying and convinced that Jesus didn't care. Only Joshua and Caleb saw promises that were bigger than giants and walled cities.

A few years ago, I found myself in a time where I was struggling to see clearly. Circumstances seemed confusing, and the actions of some close friends had been difficult to understand. It was hard to tell what was really going on inside me and around me. So I decided to take a break from my turmoil and flip on the television, just in time to catch a bit of my beloved *The Wizard of Oz*.

Dorothy's home had just been plucked out of Kansas by the tornado and crash landed in Oz. The movie was now in color; munchkins were emerging; and Glinda had just popped in on her bubble cruiser. Dorothy's eyes were wide in wonder. About the time the singing started, the Holy Spirit nudged me. "Hey, don't you think she's in a pretty good mood, considering that her house just got destroyed?"

It had never really occurred to me that she could have had a completely different reaction. Instead of awe, what if Dorothy had focused only on the awful? It would have been a completely different scene; and suddenly, I could imagine it quite clearly:

> "Hey! What's going on here?" Dorothy yells as she yanks open the tattered door and trips over Toto. "Who's responsible for this?" After walking a few steps away from the house, she turns to take in the full scope of the damage. "Are you kidding me? Isn't it bad enough that I don't have parents and am living on a rundown farm in the middle of the Dust Bowl during the Great Depression?"

About that time in my imaginary movie, the munchkins begin singing.

> "Shut up!" Dorothy screams, "I need an insurance agent . . . pronto—and you're blathering on about being off to see a wizard. Unless he's got a settlement check and a whole lot of home improvement skills, I'm not interested." There was a pause before one final shriek. "Is that a body under the house? Oh NO! That's gonna be a lawsuit for sure. Seriously, a house is dropping from the sky and you don't have enough sense to get out of the way?" Big pause. Deep sigh. "Why do these things always happen to ME?"

And then I saw the Holy Spirit's point:

Responses are choices no matter what is occurring.
And we are responsible for the choices we make.

No one makes us do anything. Anger, frustration and negativity are not unavoidable. Of course, we're all in the process of maturity, and some days are more successful than others. None of us are going to move through life without times of adversity and challenge. Jesus didn't say that in this world, we might have tribulation; He promised us that we would. However, He also gave us our response: "Cheer up, for I've overcome the world" (John 16:33, NLT). In other words, "Tough times are part of life; sometimes a very hard part of life—but compared to who I am, it's still a cause for rejoicing. Not because of what's happening, but because of who I will be for you in it."

**Our response to our circumstances is based in
identity: God's, ours, and seeing the true identity of
others.**

Jesus is the one who overcomes, and He has said that we are to be more than conquerors, through Him who loved us and gave His life for us (Romans 8:37). And how does the Holy Spirit excel in training us in this persona? He doesn't try to save us from challenges. In fact,

**God unapologetically places doors marked
"opportunity" and "offense" in close proximity to
each other and allows us to choose which we will
walk through.**

Whirlwinds of misunderstanding, poor timing, and unfortunate actions are going to occur when we're walking with other human beings, especially if we are growing quickly and taking risks together. When we find ourselves pelted by the flying debris of situations beyond our control, we may choose to run for cover or strike back at the source of our unrest. At those moments, the dust devils of swirling events will try to grow into tornadoes that create serious destruction. But devastation is not a foregone conclusion. We can anchor into who God really is, who we really are, and who we know our friends to really be—keeping everything grounded in truth when our emotions want to explode because of what seems true.

OPPORTUNITIES IN GOD

When God's true nature seems to be in contradiction to what we are experiencing, we can be offended that He isn't responding as we want Him to—or we can choose to take the opportunity of standing in who we know Him to truly be: faithful, kind, patient . . . whatever is the opposite of the offense. We will have to decide whether to create a theology of God based on our difficult experiences or based on His Word, His promises, and His true identity.

It's not enough to collect biblical truth on coffee mugs or refrigerator magnets. We're instructed to be "rooted and grounded" in it (Ephesians 3:17). The Word of God is supposed to be living, growing, and continually being more deeply established in our minds and hearts. If we've collected truth about God's identity only through academic knowledge or by just hearing someone else's experiences, we won't have developed our own revelations of His Word or the relational roots that will hold us securely in the storms of life. When what's true in our circumstances seems to be in raging conflict with the truth of who God is, it's actually an opportunity to practice our faith and become rooted in trust.

When we grow stronger because of the devil's schemes, it's a beautiful form of New Testament vengeance. This is exactly what Jesus experienced at the cross. What looked like a complete disaster for Jesus and victory for Satan, actually played right into the purposes of God.

Did the Father nail Jesus to the cross? No—but He allowed it because He saw a greater outcome than rescuing His beloved Son. Was it easy for Jesus because of that? No. Look at the Lord as He cries out in pain, feeling absolutely forsaken by the Father, asking, "Why have you abandoned Me?" (Matthew 27:46, NLT). Jesus knew the plan from before the beginning of time (1 Peter 1:19-21), so why was He questioning it now? Because under duress (and that word doesn't even come close to what the cross was for Him), it's apparently not a sin to ask God a question that you already know the answer to.

Paul wrote, "But we speak the wisdom of God in a mystery, the hidden wisdom which God ordained before the ages for our glory, which none of the rulers of this age knew; for had they known, they would not have crucified the Lord of glory. But as it is written: 'Eye has not seen, nor ear heard, nor have entered into the heart of man the things which God has prepared for those who love Him'" (1 Corinthians 2:7-9).

God has great compassion for our adversity; but He will not automatically rescue us, because He knows that what looks like utter disaster actually holds the keys to your next greatest victory.

At these moments, we will have to choose to believe that there is an opportunity to encounter God's overcoming nature—or be offended at God. Jesus was not offended at His Father on the cross, because that would have been a sin. But of all the righteous choices Jesus made throughout His lifetime, I believe that this was probably the hardest one of all. In His greatest moment of pain, He chose the opportunity for our salvation, not offense at His Father.

And not only did He resist offense, He overcame it by doing the exact opposite. He chose to trust. In His last words, Jesus completely releases His life into the seemingly invisible hands of His Father: "Into Your hands, I commit My spirit" (Luke 23:46). Christ knew the Father's true, unchanging nature and divine identity, so no matter what was occurring, it did not alter the fact that His Father's hands were the safest place to be, whether He could feel them or not.

The choice of Jesus to trust His Father on the cross is strong comfort on our most difficult days when the doors of opportunity and offense are sitting side by side, and we are allowed to choose which one we will enter.

No matter how hard it may be, the reality is that you have a champion in Jesus who really does understand completely (Hebrews 4:15) and is praying for you continually to make the most of this opportunity (Romans 8:34). Ask Him in confidence to give you wisdom (James 1:2-8) so that the trials you face don't toss you about in the waves of uncertainty in who God really is for you and to you.

GRACE WITH OURSELVES

Did you realize that you can offend yourself? It's evident in the common phrases that many of us use regularly: "I can't believe I just did that!"; "What was I thinking?"; and the classic, "When will I ever learn?" The enemy whips up a tornado of shame and rushes in with a debris cloud of self-criticism, accusation, and disappointment in our own behavior. The havoc we heap on ourselves is often greater than the condemnation of others.

We can choose to believe that we behaved that way because we are that way—or instead, understand that we have acted outside of our true identity in a way that doesn't represent who God created us to be. There's an enormous difference between the two. Our true identity in Christ is a constant, because He is never changing and lives in us. Life is about discovering the fullness of that truth and choosing to act accordingly.

When this is our perception, repentance quickly follows sin and is full of thanksgiving. We ask God to show us where the missing piece is and thank Him for giving us that part of His true nature. We're genuinely sorry, because His goodness provokes us to leave behind our lesser ways and follow His higher ones. We take the opportunity to live for righteousness, rather than continue in offense and shame over our sin.

Condemnation says that you acted badly, therefore, you are bad. Romans 8:1 says that in Christ, there is no condemnation. The conviction of the Holy Spirit allows us to feel badly when we've acted badly as a signal to stop, look, and listen. Stop and assess what's really going on here. Look and find what is missing in your experience of Jesus that would cause you to act that way. Listen to His voice encouraging you to come up higher. He's the first one to say, "You can't do that because this is who you really are, and this is who I really am for you in this place." Then we can choose to respond and go a more excellent way.

SEEING OUR FRIENDS

What about when our friends behave in ways that are not true to their Kingdom identity? We can choose disillusionment, or we can stand on the foundation of how God sees them and who we know them to truly be. Instead of, "Why are you acting like such a jerk?"—we can come alongside to remind them, "Hey, that's not who you are. This is who you really are, so you can't be doing that other stuff, my friend."

Whether it is having that perspective with another person or with ourselves, we are ever mindful that it is the goodness and kindness of God that lead us to make a different choice, to repent and go another way (Romans 2:4). Offense punishes and locks doors with condemnation, making us prisoners of our history. Conviction illuminates the truth and leads us to believe the best of our friends, while calling them up higher into their true identity, not defaulting to a lesser self.

If another person has treated us poorly, we can be offended or we can choose to embrace an opportunity to identify with Jesus, who was woefully unrecognized, misunderstood, and unappreciated during most of His life, even at times by His close friends. The Lord knows just how that feels. It doesn't mean that you need to remain in an abusive or destructive situation, but it frees you from allowing adversity or the shoddy actions of others to define who you really are.

One of the greatest relational gifts ever given to me came from a dear friend during the turmoil that prompted my *Wizard of Oz* afternoon at the beginning of this chapter. Her job placed her in a position where she was also dealing with the chaos that was swirling. In the midst of it all, I received a simple email that said, "I see you. I know you . . . and this is not you." That was it. No long explanation—just eleven words that were a lifeline and an anchor to my soul.

> **At the core of our being, all of us want to be seen for
> who we really are, so it's a good idea to sow those
> seeds into the lives of everyone we encounter.**

When God looks at us, He sees us as who we are in Christ. It's our primary identity to Him. When we are able to see others and ourselves with the same lens, we have a powerful tool to grow quickly into greater fullness of our true identity and create relationships that are deep, lasting, and impactful.

DON'T MISS THE TECHNICOLOR

Will God act in ways we don't understand? Frequently. Will people take actions that hurt our hearts? Yes. Will we do things that hurt the hearts of others? Yes. It's part of relationships on earth with God and others. And when unfortunate events occur, those two doors marked "opportunity" and "offense" are usually right before you.

Trauma, chaos, and adverse circumstances will all press to define who you are. Don't let them. You may not be able to change the situation or the people connected to them, but you can choose your response. When the tornados of life come, run into the storm cellar of your secret place with God. Don't rush out immediately to fight the tornado—because no one wins that fight.

And if the storm picks you up and deposits you in a completely unexpected landscape? Don't panic; stop and look to see where you have landed. What's here that you've never seen before? Who does God want to be for you in this place, and who can you become here that might not have been possible anywhere else?

Sometimes, in our most difficult places, our world can change from black and white to Technicolor—if we can see it. There may have been some loss, but there is usually more to be gained than we realize. Offense blinds us to the upgrades in our identity that may well be on offer. It clouds the majesty of God's kindness, faithfulness, and love that He has provided for you to encounter.

When the tornadoes of life come, choose the door marked "opportunity." The key of your true identity will open it. It's a big key on Jesus' key ring—the one He swiped from the enemy's hands (Revelation 1:18). It is an entry point to discovering that no matter what is occurring, there really is a land of opportunity that is not a fairy tale or Hollywood movie. It's a very real manifestation of life on earth from the perspective of heaven.

CHAPTER 4

UPGRADING OUR IDENTITY SOFTWARE

In 1981, I was leaving my college campus for the last time, a new graduate ready to go out into the world. I had insanely finished two degrees in three and a half years and was somewhat thankful to be leaving the academic world behind for a while. I reminisced as I wandered the corridors of the technology lab, returning various items before leaving, pausing to consider the enormous mainframe computer that had been my personal adversary. There would be no love lost between us.

My chosen field required a great deal of work with computer analyzed statistics. Because this was a very long time ago, all of my data had to be entered on a machine that punched holes in cards—a vicious contraption that excelled in jamming frequently. When the data entry was complete, the cards were banded together and handed to a technician who would run them through a mainframe computer the size of Vermont and return the results to you—two days later.

There was no way to look at the cards and know if a mistake had been made; so we were all left to wait for the results, scan them intensely and see if, by some miracle, our data entry had been flawless. If not, it was back to the punch card machine to begin the process all over again. With my level of ineptitude, both in typing and statistics, I usually started my projects a month in advance to give some thin hope that I might finish on time.

As I was feeling great elation over never having to work with this process again, I noticed a new addition to the computer lab. Along the wall were five small screens with bright green numbers appearing as students typed in their information. When I inquired about them to a fellow graduate, he sighed deeply, "Yeah, it's the latest thing that's too late for us. All of these guys will have finished in one hour what it took us three days to get done."

Thanks, Bill Gates and Steve Jobs. I really appreciate how you revolutionized technology. I sincerely do. But couldn't you have done it about four years sooner?

Those early personal computers were the beginning of a revolution, one that was hard to imagine back then. While the models I saw in 1981 bordered on the miraculous for most of us, we would soon learn that technology would accelerate at a pace that left us breathless. That 1981 wonder machine is now an antique, completely out of date. Our smart phones today hold four times that capacity!

Most of us have opened a familiar computer program and been informed that we need to download a more recent version. If you don't, then eventually your beloved operating system will no longer work properly. What was cutting edge five years ago is no longer relevant today. Holding on to old floppy disks or memory chips is futile. While they may have been extremely valuable once upon a time, that time has passed—an upgrade is needed.

The same is true for our identity. When I'm getting to know someone, I frequently listen to their language. Do they talk mostly about events in the past, or are they focused more on today and tomorrow? Are they referencing a great deal of previous history or speaking about present and future possibilities? As the conversation unfolds, I find myself wondering,

> **Are you working with a current, updated version**
> **of your Kingdom identity, or are you still trying to**
> **process your life through an outdated perspective?**

Our initial understanding of who God actually is and who He created us to be is not a one-time encounter. If it was, I would still think that the real Jesus was a cardboard cutout stuck to a flannel board in my childhood Sunday school class! Understanding our identity in Christ is an ongoing exploration where we discover new, brilliant revelations that illuminate truths we have never considered but are full of rich treasure. And as we fill up on those, we have a choice: discard the old and make room for the new or try to carry both at the same time.

TIME TO UPGRADE YOUR IDENTITY PROCESS

On our journey, we are meant to take the treasures of wisdom, trust, and God-encounters with us. Our past discoveries of life with Him are meant to fuel us forward with greater confidence into new places. But what other bits and pieces are we carrying with us that have become outdated?

What old thoughts about God and ourselves are we still bringing with us just in case we mistakenly think we might need them?

Old technology isn't like fine furniture or rare coins. It doesn't increase in value just because it's old. Not everything gets better with age. When your computer fatally fails, you get rid of it. It died; and when it did, it was no longer relevant or useful.

"Set your mind on things above, not on things on the earth. For you died, and your life is hidden with Christ in God. When Christ who is our life appears, then you also will appear with Him in glory" (Colossians 3:2-4).

Our old ways of thinking about God and ourselves are meant to be continually upgraded as more and more of our life with Christ is revealed. This isn't just a verse about heaven one day. Christ in us is our hope of glory in this life (Colossians 1:27). As Jesus was in this world, so are we to be (1 John 4:17). But it's a perception that is only visible when we share the same heavenly view point as God's.

We can't process our New Man identity in Christ through an outdated system of old covenant beliefs.

If you are in a time where God is revealing Himself as your peace, those thoughts can only be transformationally processed through a filter of grace, kindness, and joy. You will have many opportunities to see the events of your life from His elevated perspective, encounter His gorgeous patience, and be surrounded with His empowering presence. Like Dorothy in Oz, a new world can potentially open up before you, full of possibilities and promise, even in a time where circumstances are chaotic or previous securities have crashed. We can't effectively practice peace, rest, or patience when everything is going smoothly. The world can be a place of difficulty, sorrow, hardship, and heartache—but our joy is found in knowing that our life is hidden with the One who faced all those challenges, overcame them, and now intercedes on our behalf to do the same (Ephesians 1:20 and Romans 8:34).

But if your old perception system of failure, frustration, and fear is still in place, occasions to encounter peace can be misinterpreted as your inability to prevent them from happening or respond well when they occur. Our outdated perspective may default to worry, problem solving, and shame. Instead of giving ourselves the same vast measure of grace that God uses with us, we pick up the heavy weights of condemnation and victim-thinking that leave us wondering why this is happening to us—again.

CALL KINGDOM SUPPORT

God's empowering grace to see ourselves as He does positions us to overcome, if not quickly, then always eventually. When we have hit a challenging place, we are meant to look into the mirror of His true nature and see the soft, confident eyes of Jesus looking back at us. He knows in whom we've believed and is joyfully convinced of His ability to transform our image into His. When our behavior doesn't align with our best self in Christ, He knows that it will be His goodness that encourages us to stop, look, and listen for a more excellent way. After that, it is just a matter of doing what He asked His disciples to do on the first day He met them: "Follow Me." Follow those wonderful eyes and that voice that continually whispers, "I know. I've been there but you are my beloved one and nothing can change that." He restores our souls and leads in a righteous way, for His wonderful name's sake (Hebrews 4:15; Jeremiah 31:3; Psalm 23:3).

It's a mindset that is a continuing journey in my life. Before I met the real Jesus, my primary operating system for life was based on performance for acceptance. If I did well, I was good and, therefore, acceptable to God. If I did not do well, I felt I had disappointed God and was no longer a good child of His. It is a rare occasion where that old thinking tries to reboot itself in my life, but that's mostly because God loves to arrange occasions for me to be reminded just how dead that old way of perceiving life really is.

My favorite so far occurred last year when a snappy pop-up window on my computer promised to upgrade my processing speed. It looked authentic, so I clicked on it. Without investigating further, I signed up for the instant service that promised to protect me and my computer—only to discover that I didn't just get a new program, I got all the adware, malware, and a whole host of other "wares" that quickly took over my operating system.

It wasn't a virus, just a bad idea. Before long, there was a number to call on my screen that promised to help, but instead, it connected me to a very insistent foreign man who sharply declared that all of my information was about to be destroyed if I did not give him control of my computer immediately. When I said I wanted more information before proceeding, he forcefully countered, "Who else do you know? Who do you know that can help you now?"

Well, certainly not this guy—and I hung up.

My next call? My first ever to the authentic support team for my brand of computer, where I confessed my complete ignorance—and waited for the condescending tone of the expert who is worn out from endless days of talking with not-so-bright people like me.

But that wasn't at all what happened. I met Daniel.

When I told Daniel the product I had purchased, his first response was, "I'm so sorry. That has probably not been a fun experience for you." Maybe he didn't hear right. I did this, Daniel. I did this ridiculous action of my own free will. Aren't you at least going to give me a well-deserved lecture?

No, he wasn't. Instead, he continued, "Hey, no worries. I have become a champ at this one, because lots of folks have done this. I'll help you get this mess taken care of, show you some new nifty things about your computer, and get your security improved so that it doesn't happen again."

And he did.

With a couple of clicks, he was able to see my screen and showed me what to do. He walked me through every step and told me how it worked. During the long pauses while my computer had to reboot a couple of times, we chatted about the funny aspects of technology. And thirty minutes later, my problem wasn't just solved, but my computer was safer, and I was significantly wiser. And for all of that stellar service there was no charge. "This one's on me" was his reply.

After I hung up the phone, it struck me: Encountering Daniel was like encountering the nature of the Holy Spirit.

How many times have I opened my mind and heart to things that seemed true but were not the truth? The myriad of occasions where I entertained a thought that was not pure, peaceable, or full of good fruit about myself or others, and then it took root and began to spread into a mindset that wasn't like the true nature of God at all—invading my perceptions and warping my perspectives.

That justifiable judgment or self-centered opinion seemed pretty harmless at first, until it became more pervasive—at which point I wanted to change my mind. So I would try really, really hard not to think like that, but in focusing on the negative, it only seemed to expand. All I encountered was the condemnation and threats of the accuser who wanted to say, "Who is going to help you now? After all, *you* let this in!"

I didn't need to be shamed into focusing harder on my sin in order to stop it. I needed to repent toward the aspect of God's nature that would overcome it instead. It wasn't about emptying out old behavior but filling up on God's authentic truth, until there simply was no room or fuel for the old mindsets to exist.

Repentance: It's like calling "Kingdom Support."

The Holy Spirit answers with a peace-filled voice and listens when we say we are sorry. He is not going to tell you what is wrong with you but what's missing, and He will assure you that He is an expert in providing it. He is the Teacher and the Helper here to instruct us in the right way to go when we get off track (Isaiah 30:21). And when He's finished, we discover that God has already paid the price.

Our responsibility is to call, ask, and receive.

When we have sinned—acted poorly, opened the door to a negative perspective, or been less than who God created us to be—we usually know we messed up. Heaps of condemnation only bury us further, and it is not from Him (Romans 8:1). The Holy Spirit turns on the Light and convicts us with goodness, knowing it's the only real path to choosing to repent and go a different way. "Or do you despise the riches of His goodness, forbearance, and longsuffering, not knowing that the goodness of God leads you to repentance?" (Romans 2:4). His kindness opens our hearts and we feel safe—not afraid. There is no fear in love, and God is love (1 John 4:8).

Like talking with Daniel, we leave our times of divine conversation with Him feeling more brilliant, not less. God has walked us through the steps of our own unique process to trash the lies that need to go and to download His truth that will take us higher. We are able to tell Him how truly sorry we are and hear Him say, "I know. I appreciate that—and I've got it covered. Now let's see what I have here that can fill that place instead." We will end the encounter actually better than we were before—more protected, not just back to normal.

Is all of this a rather simplistic way of looking at an infinite God? In many ways, yes. The Holy Spirit's power and the depths of the love of Christ go far, far beyond such a simple comparison. But once again, the Jesus that used mustard seeds and fig trees loves to hide truth in the midst of our everyday lives.

IDENTITY UPGRADES NEEDED?

How long has it been since you have taken some time to ask the Lord, "How do You see me?" and then allowed time for Him to respond? It's a simple question that He adores answering. It is why there are opportunities for you to have those conversations in the guidebook that comprises the second half of this book. Often, our lives race along, and we find ourselves in new territory that requires a fresh perspective on who we are with God. Our previous experiences may have been good, but every new level of life in God will require us to upgrade our identity of Him and of ourselves with Him.

None of us want to develop monument mindsets about our identity: moments in time that we freeze and hold on to. They can be memorials to our last great victory 20 years ago or markers of bitter defeat that we don't feel we can move beyond. No one point on our journey defines us completely. It was a truth that Paul knew well. "Brethren, I do not count myself to have apprehended; but one thing I do, forgetting those things which are behind and reaching forward to those things which are ahead, I press toward the goal for the prize of the upward call of God in Christ Jesus. Therefore let us, as many as are mature, have this mind; and if in anything you think otherwise, God will reveal even this to you" (Philippians 3:13-15).

As we travel through life, our true identity in Christ appears and becomes more clear and heaven-based than earth-bound. Like Paul, we're discarding the old perceptions that no longer serve us well: always moving forward, always rising higher toward fullness of life in Christ, understanding and encountering more of who He really is and who you really are in Him.

CHAPTER 5

FREEDOM FROM DOING IT ALL

Now then, we are ambassadors for Christ, as though God were pleading through us: we implore you on Christ's behalf, be reconciled to God.

2 CORINTHIANS 5:20

One of our primary roles as ambassadors of the Kingdom is to demonstrate God's goodness and kindness in such a powerful manner that people are drawn to Jesus. Every day, there are endless opportunities to do this: food and health services, visiting inmates, neighborhood gatherings, prayer teams, missions, child care, assistance for the homeless and elderly—so many ways to express the goodness and kindness of God that He has asked us to do. Then there's developing the gifts that God has given us in areas such as teaching, music, speaking, writing, leadership, administration and many, many more.

So how do we differentiate between what is a good idea and a God idea?

Writers far and wide have pondered the question of purpose. I've always loved Mark Twain's observation that "The two most important days in your life are the day you are born and the day you find out why." Though we would probably add the day that we come to know Jesus as an important day, this thought highlights that just being born (and even being born again) is not the only part of our identity. What we choose to do in this life is a significant part of how our truest identity manifests on earth.

NEED-BASED VS. IDENTITY-BASED RESPONSES

The world can seem so vast and the needs are so great that it can be easier to do nothing than to try to sort out where to start. "What can one man do?" paralysis tries to turn us into couch potatoes. Those who do venture off the couch are often faced with a different fight. Suddenly, every good, well-meaning opportunity seems to pile up on the front porch, pounding on the door shouting, "Choose me! Choose me!"

The world resounds with "We need you," and many sincere believers with servant hearts say yes; however, need can never be the determining factor in what you say yes or no to, because the needs of this world are endless. Reasonable service is an authentic part of life in God, and we want to joyfully help others whenever we can. However, fear of unmet needs can never be its motivation. When it is, a slippery slope of guilt leads many to say yes out of obligation alone. While the need may be temporarily filled, the volunteers often lack longevity. Without the joy of the Lord in His assignments for us, we are disconnected from our primary source of strength and our stamina fails.

What we do in this life must be a joyful response to our identity in who God is for us, in us, and through us. These are our Kingdom assignments.

In Acts 3, Peter and John did not respond to the requested need. The lame man was only hoping for money, but they chose to give him something from the power of their relationship with God the Healer instead. "Then Peter said, 'Silver and gold I do not have, but what I do have I give you: In the name of Jesus Christ of Nazareth, rise up and walk'" (Acts 3:6).

Jesus did the same thing with the man who had confined his possibilities to a random angelic event. "When Jesus saw him lying there, and knew that he already had been in that condition a long time, He said to him, 'Do you want to be made well?' The sick man answered Him, 'Sir, I have no man to put me into the pool when the water is stirred up; but while I am coming, another steps down before me.' Jesus said to him, 'Rise, take up your bed and walk.' And immediately the man was made well, took up his bed, and walked" (John 5:6-9).

The Lord could have just picked the man up and put him in the pool, but instead He responded from who He knew the Father wanted to be for this man: his Healer.

JESUS WORKED IN KINGDOM ASSIGNMENTS

Jesus was the architect of this wisdom during His earthly experience. "Most assuredly, I say to you, the Son can do nothing of Himself, but what He sees the Father do; for whatever He does, the Son also does in like manner" (John 5:19). Put that together with 1 John 4:17, "As He is, so are we in this world," and we have a pretty definitive answer to the ever-present question, "What do you think I should do?" Well, what do you love to do, and is the Father doing that too?

"What are my Kingdom assignments?" is not a functional question. It's a relational one.

Jesus' wisdom in John 5:19 takes all of the pressure off. If Jesus was only required to follow His Father's lead, then so can we. In fact, isn't that the first instruction that He gave His disciples? "Follow me, and I will make you fishers of men" (Matthew 4:19). The Lord didn't lure them with extensive details of the job, or even something that sounded sensible—instead, He asked them to follow Him. If they wanted to know Him, they had to go where He was going. Jesus was following His Father; the disciples were following Him. The Lord wasn't just making a onetime offer, nor was it about starting a ministry where they clocked out at 5:00 p.m. He was offering a life with Him, traveling and eating together, visiting homes, inns, and occasionally, a synagogue or two. Life with Jesus would always be about following where He was going and training them to do what He was doing. It still is.

Our joyful intentionality is connected to our relationship with God, which inspires us to action. When people are floundering in uncertainty as to their Kingdom assignments, I usually will not engage in much of a discussion until after they've spent some time in worship and soaking in just how much God adores them. Jesus talked often with His Father and was deeply grounded in His affection. Christ knew who His Dad really was; and, therefore, He knew His own identity and what He was meant to do in His lifetime.

KNOWING GOD'S IDENTITY OPENS UP OUR OWN

We see it most clearly on His last night before the cross in John 13:3-5: "Jesus, knowing that the Father had given all things into His hands, and that He had come from God and was going to God, rose from supper and laid aside His garments, took a towel and girded Himself. After that, He poured water into a basin and began to wash the disciples' feet, and to wipe them with the towel with which He was girded." Jesus knew who He had come from, and He knew who He was going back to. From that rock-solid knowledge, He served His friends.

As we understand God's identity more clearly, we will better comprehend who He created us to be and the Kingdom assignments that He has for us to do.

Once again, Peter is a great example of this. While his friends are making random guesses as to the identity of Jesus based on the latest opinion polls, the Father connects with the revelation that quite possibly had been growing in Peter's heart for a while. In the inspiration of that divine conversation, the Father breathes life on that spark, and Peter suddenly has eyes to see something that he has never seen clearly before: "He [Jesus] said to them, 'But who do you say that I am?' Simon Peter answered and said, 'You are the Christ, the Son of the living God.' Jesus answered and said to him, 'Blessed are you, Simon Bar-Jonah, for flesh and blood has not revealed this to you, but My Father who is in heaven.'"

But that's not the end of this exchange. Jesus continues, " I also say to you that you are Peter, and on this rock I will build My church, and the gates of Hades shall not prevail against it. And I will give you the keys of the kingdom of heaven, and whatever you bind on earth will be bound in heaven, and whatever you loose on earth will be loosed in heaven" (Matthew 16:15-19).

I used to think that this event was one in which the impetuous Peter blurts out the true identity of the Christ in a random moment—but I'm not so sure anymore. I've come to read this passage in a very different way now. What if it was actually a very quiet exchange while the other disciples were making their various guesses? What if Peter didn't shout out his answer? What if he looked directly into Jesus' eyes, and for the first time, he saw Him—*really* saw Him? What if the revelation was so powerful, it took Peter's breath away and all he could do was whisper in amazement, "You are the Christ, the son of the living God." And in a moment of time, a rock-solid revelation was birthed inside of him.

If so, I imagine Jesus seeing the light come on in Peter's spirit, as they looked at each other in this new relational space. The rest of the disciples may have still been shouting out their guesses, but Jesus and Peter wouldn't have heard them. A deeply satisfied smile might have begun to appear on the Lord's face, as He watched a currently unredeemed man connect with His spirit of wisdom and revelation on earth as it was in heaven.

And from that place, Jesus could speak to Peter about his true identity in a way that had not been possible before. Once again, the door was opening to a new level of relationship between God and man that had been dreamed of for eternity. It wasn't going to stay open for Peter yet. He would forget a few more times. It would take the cross and the invasion of the Holy Spirit for true transformation to occur. But it was a preview, a glimpse into how the Kingdom was meant to work. God shows us who He really is; and when the eyes of our heart are enlightened to see the way God sees (Ephesians 1:18), He can talk to us in a new way about who we really are, what we are created to do in this life, and the authority of heaven that will back us up. It will be the foundation on which He can build—not only individually, but corporately.

MOVING FORWARD IN CONFIDENCE

In our identity as His beloved ones, we want to live with an ever-present sense of God's permission. We trust His promise that we will hear His voice behind us, pointing out the path if we get off track (Isaiah 30:21), so we can move confidently forward as seems best to us and the Holy Spirit, with hearts that are joyfully sensitive to redirection if it's needed. If we find ourselves afraid to move for fear of failure or making a mistake, then we have an upgrade in perfect love to encounter; for there is no fear in love, and God is love itself.

I don't stress about missing God because I trust Him. I remember in the early days of sorting speaking invitations, I dutifully sat down to embark on listening for which were my assignments and which were not, only to have Him laughingly say, "Sweetheart, all of them are training. Just say yes to them all." My primary assignment during those two years was to go anywhere I was asked, if my schedule permitted, and garner a wide array of experience. Sometimes, it is as simple as that.

For the other occasions, I've developed a quick list of identity based questions when I'm considering my opportunities: What aspect of my identity does this opportunity connect to? Do I have promises, key scriptures or prophetic words that will resource me here or that this opportunity will allow me to step into?

If I feel that the choice before me is an accurate expression of who God created me to be or would be good training for a future destiny, then I will be more likely to consider it further. If I don't hear anything and still feel peaceful, I keep moving forward with more questions:

> **Who does He want to be for the people extending the**
> **invitation? Who does the Lord want to be for me in**
> **this place? Will I need to upgrade my identity to take**
> **this assignment?**

If these spark a sense of interest and partnership with the Lord, I'm likely to say yes. But if the invitation is in an area that doesn't connect directly with my primary passions, I'm happy to recommend someone else. I highly value many aspects of Kingdom life and joyfully participate in them when the opportunity arises—but it doesn't mean they are a primary assignment or that I'm the best person to teach on that subject. When we're working in an area of Kingdom assignment, it is our passion, vision, and relationship with God that people respond to, just as much as it is the content of our teaching.

FREEDOM FROM HAVING TO DO IT ALL

Christ did not meet all the needs He ever encountered because He wasn't intended to in His earthly ministry. He only did what He saw His Father doing. Jesus modeled His dependency on the Father and His trust in the Holy Spirit to be our Teacher and Helper, empowering believers to heal the sick, raise the dead, cast out devils, and carry out the work of the Kingdom (Matthew 10:8).

Jesus did amazing works, but He clearly tells us that there are even greater works for us to do (John 14:12). So the answer to "What should I be doing?" seems to be to let people know that the Kingdom of heaven is within their reach—demonstrate it, and just do it more than Jesus did. But do it how He did it: by being in such a close relationship with His Father that all He had to do and say was what His Father was doing and saying. Nothing more—and nothing less. Together, they create the greatest expressions of the greatest commandments: to love God most and love each other (Matthew 22:36-40).

Explore the Kingdom to find where your piece fits best for now, and then do it with all of your heart. Maybe it's your ultimate destiny, but most likely it's part of your training. It makes no difference to God if it's caring for your family or serving in a foreign country. If it's an aspect of who He created you to be, you'll be in the right place to either manifest your destiny or be preparing for it.

VALUE BASED CHOICES

Your Kingdom assignments in this life may not always conform to earthly norms, but they should always align with God's values that are meant to govern our lives. Our actions are meant to be founded on relational values that reflect our passion for God and people, rather than raw obedience to a long list of obligatory good works.

First Corinthians 13:4-8 exemplifies this clearly. I particularly like the version found in the Amplified Bible: "Love endures with patience and serenity, love is kind and thoughtful, and is not jealous or envious; love does not brag and is not proud or arrogant. It is not rude; it is not self-seeking, it is not provoked [nor overly sensitive and easily angered]; it does not take into account a wrong endured. It does not rejoice at injustice, but rejoices with the truth [when right and truth prevail]. Love bears all things [regardless of what comes], believes all things [looking for the best in each one], hopes all things [remaining steadfast during difficult times], endures all things [without weakening]. Love never fails [it never fades nor ends]."

The behavior described here is the result of valuing love because God is love itself (1 John 4:8). It's easy to say, "Love God. Love each other," but how does that manifest in everyday life? Well, 1 Corinthians 13 gives us a pretty good idea. It's not because of keeping these as rules, but because we've encountered God to be like this with us and are now reflecting that in the actions we choose to take with others.

Without valuing what God values, and doing lots of good things like giving away all your possessions and sacrificing your life, does no good at all (1 Corinthians 13:3). God values love above all else, as well as joy, peace, patience, kindness, gentleness, goodness, and self-control.

Our values for what God values impact not only what we will do but how we will do it. Our Kingdom assignments will be the specific ways in which we express what God values to the world around us. As we behold these qualities in Him, we will naturally express them within any assignment that is ours. Our language and actions will mirror who we've encountered Him to be. We're loving, kind, peaceful, gentle, etc., because He's been that way to us.

SHIFTING FROM SPOTLIGHTS TO LASERS

Kingdom assignments, combined with living from God's values, can bring focus when there are a lot of good opportunities to choose from. A spotlight is an intense beam that can be seen for miles. But a laser, which is also light, is so powerfully focused that it can cut through steel or be precise enough to do surgery. Both are forms of light, but focus brings power and impact.

Jesus told us that we were to be the light of the world, set in a visible place for all to see (Matthew 5:14). There's certainly a place for Christians to be broadly brilliant, but I also believe that when we focus on our Kingdom assignments, we become lasers that can break through any obstacle. We know who God will be for us and for those around us in a way that is highly impactful. Our words and work become arrows to the target rather than scattered bits of shrapnel.

As ambassadors of the Kingdom, we discover our assignments as we travel. Opportunities appear, and we must choose whether they are for us or not. Are they in line with our identity and passions? Remember, "All things work together for good" has two conditions—"to those who love God, to those who are called according to His purpose" (Romans 8:28). Is this part of His purpose for us? If so, we can connect with

His joy for us in it. Whether it's taking care of children or an elderly parent, pastoring a church or running a corporation, there's a sense of being on target if it's the work God has created you to do. Notice, I didn't say that it makes it easy all the time, but there is a sense of ease in it because you're aligned with your true identity in Christ.

WHEN KINGDOM ASSIGNMENTS END

When work in one of our assignments ends, we don't lose our sense of identity, because it's not the work that defines us. Rather, it is who we are that brought life to the work. We're free to move about the Kingdom, contributing our pieces and rejoicing in the work of others who are contributing theirs. As one of my dearest friends often reminds me, "We can't get it all together; but together we can get it all."

I've had some Kingdom assignments end suddenly in a moment of divine intervention and a profound knowledge that God said I was done. Once, a member of my current ministry group was sharing something that she was not particularly happy about, and I realized that I could no longer understand her words. As her voice actually receded into a version of Charlie Brown's teacher ("Waa waa waa"), the Lord simply said, "This isn't your job anymore." It stunned me—but I instantly knew He was right. I took a few days to let it all sink in pray, and then began the necessary steps of faith to finish that season with an amazing group of women. I was prepared because I had been well-trained as a leader. I always had several people whom I was raising up so that the ministry never depended on my presence alone. When I said my good-byes, I had no idea what would come next—but within a month, a new opportunity emerged.

On other occasions, it's been a gentle sense that a season was coming to a close. Two years before I took early retirement from my job as an elementary school teacher, I knew that my timeline was no longer God's. I first recognized it when a last-minute change to my room assignment occurred two days before school began. Without warning, I had to leave behind the room that I had spent all of my 18-year career in—but instead of being sad, I was oddly energized. As I took down beloved treasures made by children whose children I was now teaching, I was overwhelmed with gratitude. And then I realized, I wasn't going to be a classroom teacher for much longer. It wasn't immediate, but within a couple of years, it was indeed time to move on. My plan had been to teach for 30-plus years, and it's probably still true. It was just that after 20 years, it was no longer to be with children.

Often, God allows us to practice letting go of the
assignments we have adored so that we can be trusted

**with the more expansive ones ahead. He loves us
enough to not allow our identity to become too
closely tied to our ministry or occupation.**

I'm sure there are people who have an authentic reason for staying in the same place and the same position for decades, but if you cannot name at least two people who could easily step up if you step out—you might want to have a chat with the Holy Spirit about that one. It's a statement that's said with kindness, but also with conviction. A key assignment of any Kingdom leader is to create opportunities for those around them. Imagine if your job or ministry role ended tomorrow. Have you invested in someone to expand the work you started? How many leaders have you brought up to your level of leadership or have entrusted to further develop a work you once pioneered?

The mentors who raised me have probably lost count of the people they have launched. They did not look for servants to their Kingdom assignments but became catalysts to ours. I hope I can surpass their mark, but it will be a tall order to fill. I just know that actively bringing up other people into their destiny is a huge priority to me and one of my highest values in leadership.

**When your ministry or work has become your
identity, your own growth will be extremely
limited—and so will anyone working with you.**

At the end of it all, it's a journey of faith. Knowing our Kingdom assignments is a great compass, but God is the one who orders our steps. He's made the instructions pretty simple, "Follow Me," and so we do. I believe this relational process sensitizes us to knowing when Kingdom assignments are beginning—and ending— because it was born out of a divine conversation of identity in the first place.

CHAPTER 6

THE CURRENCY OF IDENTITY

You've just walked onto a fancy car lot, ready to trade in that old dented junker for a new, fully loaded Ferrari. You choose your model and color, reviewing the engine specs, just as the salesman approaches. After an hour discussing the various advantages of each option, you sit down to negotiate the deal. Then comes the question that every buyer must be able to answer: "How are you going to pay for this?"

Just wildly wanting this amazing car in Azzurro Metallic Blue isn't enough to make the dealership hand over the keys. As you may have noticed, financial institutions require tangible proof of income. Your future plans to get rich quick won't qualify you for the purchase. To get your dream car, you'll need to have the cash.

In the Kingdom, God's promises are our currency. They are the absolute commitments from an unchangeable God that resource our identity and our destiny. But as with the finances for a large purchase, it's wise not to wait until you need the funds to accumulate them. A shrewd investor saves and works with his money. A savvy businesswoman understands value when she sees it and invests for the future.

Every aspect of our identity has a promise attached to it—a scripture, a prophetic word, or other God encounter. These promises hold the favor that fuels our development and training as we grow into the fullness of everything God created us to be. But as with any inheritance, we need to actively partner with God so that when the time comes to step up into the next level of our identity, our personal promise experiences have produced the faith and trust required.

PROMISES EXPAND WHEN VALUED

While God gives His promises freely, it is our engagement with them that causes the power of our promises to multiply and grow. Money that is buried in the ground has worth but no impact. It is our interactive experiences with these valuable truths, not just our knowledge of their existence, that allows our confidence, trust, and courage to expand. Like the wise servants in Matthew 25, we want to treat our promises like the precious currency that they are in the Kingdom—invest wisely and position ourselves to have outstanding equity in the Spirit when challenges arise or new opportunities become evident.

Scripture is filled with promises. It's literally a treasure chest waiting to be opened and explored. Peter spoke of the quality of our promises when he wrote, "as His divine power has given to us all things that pertain to life and godliness, through the knowledge of Him who called us by glory and virtue, by which have been given to us exceedingly great and precious promises, that through these you may be partakers of the divine nature, having escaped the corruption that is in the world through lust" (2 Peter 1:3-4). These promises are described as "exceedingly great and precious," not mediocre suggestions of what God might do if He happens to be in a good mood. They're expansive, covering every aspect of godly life, and as such, deserve to be highly regarded and cared for. Promises are something to be valued!

GEMS OF PROMISE

My mother understood the value of her promises, and she had a unique way of expressing it. On her coffee table was a crystal bowl filled with large, beautiful glass gems. In the morning, the sun would stream in and fill the room with a rainbow. Beside it sat a little red leather book of God's promises, and from time to time, she would hold the book and ask the Lord, "What's Your jewel for me today?" Then she would open her book and discover her promise. My mother had an amazing sense of wonder for Scripture, and while this seemed like such a simple thing to do, time and again God used it powerfully in both of our lives.

What I loved most was that when she had found a scripture promise "gem," she didn't let it go. She would select a glass stone from her crystal bowl and set it on the table by itself. "That's so I will think about that promise every time I walk by, because it will either help me today or will be just what I need tomorrow." Sometimes the table would have four or five gems sitting out, and if asked, my mother could tell you what the promise was for each. When I noticed that a stone had been put back into the bowl, I could be sure there was a story behind it—an occasion when that very promise was fulfilled by God.

As she grew less able in her final year, there were a lot more gems on the table next to the oxygen supplies and medications. On the first morning after she had peacefully gone to be with Jesus, I sat on her couch at dawn as the sunlight poured through her crystal bowl. A rainbow of colors filled the room—and then I realized: all the stones had been returned. Despite the many difficult circumstances that had tried to indicate otherwise, God had indeed kept all of His promises to her till the end. There were no jewels of promise still waiting to be fulfilled.

Of the numerous truths that my mother's relationship with God taught me, one of the most enduring lessons was considering our promises as "exceedingly great and precious." She treated them with care and confidence. No challenge was ever met head on. Her first action was always to check her bank account of promises. Though she never said it in exactly these words, when difficult news arrived, she always communicated a sense of "Just a minute—I know I have a promise for that." It was never trite or contrived. It was her reality from a life of experiencing God's faithfulness. His nature could be absolutely trusted, and if He had made a promise, then His failure to keep that promise was never an option to her. Promises are one of our great inheritances from the Lord, and how to treasure them has certainly been one of the wonderful riches my mother left to me.

IDENTITY HAS PROMISES ATTACHED

Every aspect of our identity that emerges will have a promise attached to it. That promise often comes through scriptures or "Inheritance Words"—those verses that leap off the page and come to life at key moments in our lives. But our promises can also be found in the words God speaks to our hearts and through prophetic words given by others. No matter how you discover them, they are there!

In the exploration of our truest identity, it is vital that we identify, collect, value, and invest the promises that emerge. Not only are they a resource for our growth, but they are a powerful weapon when we are challenged by negativity, the harsh opinions of others or our own lack. Promises are the chief agent for converting problems into possibilities. Instead of seeing through a lens of "Satan is attacking me" or "I'm really struggling with this," promises encourage us to embrace the situation as a training ground for becoming more firmly established in the truth of God's solemn pledges to His word. The best time to practice a promise is under fire. And it infuriates our adversary when the events he's orchestrated to frustrate, dishearten, or defeat you are the very ones you decide to use as "promise practice." It's a brilliant strategy for getting him to cease and desist.

Paul knew the power of promises, and he encouraged his young, dear friend Timothy to utilize them to their fullest potential. "This command I entrust to you, Timothy, my son, in accordance with the prophecies previously made concerning you, that by them you fight the good fight, keeping faith and a good conscience, which some have rejected and suffered shipwreck in regard to their faith" (1 Timothy 1:18-19 NASB). Our words of promise are weapons that allow us to overcome when what seems true wants to overtake what is true. We can't afford to just roll over in those times. It would be like abandoning the bridge of a ship at the height of the storm, allowing for needless shipwreck. It's a powerful act of spiritual warfare to stand in peace and say, "Lord, You said . . ." Sometimes, we may begin with tears, but as we continue in thanksgiving, our words gain strength until whispered promises become steady, formidable declarations.

FULLY PRESENT IN FAITH OR FEELINGS

It's important to note that words of promise often rely on faith rather than feelings. God is fully present in both because (you guessed it) He promised that He would never leave us nor abandon us (Hebrews 13:5). When our emotions don't seem to connect to our comprehension, we can pray with thanksgiving that this promise is true and embrace the opportunity to trust. It's a key reason that God pledged to give us peace that was powerful enough to bypass our understanding (Philippians 4:7). Facts and feelings are not guaranteed. God's presence is.

Faith is often an act of the will, a result of joyful intentionality in choosing to believe that God meant what He said. Jesus did it as He prayed in Gethsemane. He directly said that it was not His will to continue on and was willing to consider other options. It's the real meaning of the classic scripture, "Father, if it is Your will, take this cup away from Me; nevertheless not My will, but Yours, be done" (Luke 22:42). We can all be eternally grateful that Jesus chose the Father's will over His own—but it was clearly a powerful choice made through faith, not feelings.

OUTCOMES, NOT OBJECTIVES

The astonishing news is that we never have to try to have more faith in God's promises! It's not an objective; it's a natural outcome of a deep and abiding relationship with the Lord where we know and have encountered His true identity. Hope, trust, courage, and faith: all of these are outcomes, not end goals in and of themselves.

We can't try harder to have more. When we know the true nature of God, we'll be at peace, fully trusting that He is well able to express Himself as the Great Overcomer. It was another admonition Paul made to Timothy: "For this reason I also suffer these things; nevertheless I am not ashamed, for I know whom I have believed and am persuaded that He is able to keep what I have committed to Him until that Day" (2 Timothy 1:12). Paul trusted the wonder-filled, living knowledge of the God he adored; so even though it was a time of suffering, he was at rest (Philippians 3:10).

> **Our job is not to create exceedingly great and**
> **precious promises. That's been done and they are**
> **already given to us. Our responsibility is to hold on**
> **to them.**

The enemy can't overcome God's promises, so his only hope is to deceive you into letting go of them. "Therefore do not cast away your confidence, which has great reward. For you have need of endurance, so that after you have done the will of God, you may receive the promise" (Hebrews 10:35-36). Our confidence is in knowing the true identity of who we've believed in so that we don't toss out our promises in the trash can of poor circumstances.

PROMISES RELEASE PROCESS

All promises release a process of beholding and becoming. We don't transform into the fullness of their reality overnight, but we can be confident that the One who began this good work in us will also be the One who walks with us to its completion (Philippians 1:6). We're encouraged to stay engaged in developing our promises from concept to reality, and God tells us directly that it's a process that requires two primary things: faith and patience. "And we desire that each one of you show the same diligence to the full assurance of hope until the end, that you do not become sluggish, but imitate those who through faith and patience inherit the promises" (Hebrews 6:11-12).

Our role is to hold on to what God has said and believe that He meant it. We release our timetables into His eternal hands, waiting actively, with expectancy and patience, knowing that the outcome will be well worth it. There's no assurance that it will be easy or quick. Remember what Psalm 105:19 said of Joseph: "Until the time that his word came to pass, the word of the Lord tested him." The Amplified Bible says, ". . . tested and refined him." Promises are the pure gold of God's Word, but all gold requires a refining process; so why consider it a surprise? As we talked about before, at the end of Joseph's story, we can see the perfect timing of God that not only saved his family, but all of Egypt and the surrounding nations in a time of famine. But when Joseph was sold into slavery by his brothers or when he landed in an Egyptian prison unjustly accused, those promise must have seemed very dim. Those words tested and refined Joseph, but he never let go of them. As the years passed, he gained the skills, wisdom, character, and understanding that would be required to run a powerful nation, though there was no sign that all of his difficulties were preparing him for that destiny.

I've learned in the past year that claiming an inheritance in real life requires more than waltzing into the bank and collecting an amount. Even with a well-prepared family, there's a lot of paperwork, real estate to prepare and sell, phone calls to make, notaries to visit, and paperwork. (Did I mention the paperwork?) So, should I have discontinued the process just because it was challenging? Of course not. An inheritance is a gift from those who loved you, and they worked hard to provide it. You don't walk away from that!

Our promises are the same. God has fully paid for our inheritance in Christ. A death occurred in the family of God, and we became the richer for it. But an inheritance must be appropriated. We have a new birth certificate at salvation that makes us a member of the family, fully qualified to inherit these exceedingly great and precious promises, but it requires our engagement to allocate them in our lives. Otherwise, they sit in a spiritual vault, still retaining all of their value but remaining unclaimed and without impact.

WHAT'S ALREADY IN YOUR ACCOUNT?

When adversity occurs, we're often prone to believe that the answer is "out there" somewhere, when it is often already in our possession. God is frequently giving us promises, prophecies, and Inheritance Words before we need them because He knows what is coming—and He has given us our provision ahead of time. That's why our first movement in any difficulty should be to step back rather than to run forward. As my mother exemplified, a good first question is, "Wait a minute; what's my promise for this?"

That wisdom has saved me more times than I can remember, but one of the most powerful encounters was during a difficult season that combined some really spectacular ministry and business challenges, along with an interesting health diagnosis. For several months, my chest had felt very tight and was sometimes painful. I figured that I should probably get it checked out. After a plethora of truly adventurous medical tests (one of which involved a nuclear canister, a treadmill, and a guy in a hazmat suit), my lovely doctors decided that I had a very stiff heart muscle that apparently would get even stiffer as the years progressed. It has a long fancy name, but the eventual prognosis was less than stellar.

The cardiologist's presentation was very kind, but it wouldn't have mattered. That exquisite peace that passes understanding wrapped beautifully around me as I listened. I didn't have any questions; I only wanted to finish up so that I could find a quiet spot to rest, be still, and begin to listen.

I knew that the answer wasn't one to be sought out there somewhere, nor was it time to call 57 friends and get their opinion. I wasn't sure what to pray yet, but I was certain that the answer was in my collected promises—but where? None of them sprung to life for me, so I waited, knowing that at the right moment, the treasure would appear.

As I began a long drive about a week later, I found myself immersed in worship. My spirit quickened; and suddenly, as the music broadened, I could hear pounding hooves and found myself envisioning a scene from a recent film about Secretariat.[iv] Years ago, I had been given a prophetic word that my life was like his: a fearless, joyful champion, built for both speed and endurance.

In one of the final scenes of the movie, this magnificent horse is rounding the last turn of the Belmont Stakes and the grueling final race of the Triple Crown. As many people know, he won that race by an otherworldly 31 lengths in a record time that remains unbroken today. At the moment when he should have been the most tired and was under the most pressure, he was at his best. I'd read the story years before, but now the recent film joined this iconic moment in time with the verses of Job 39:19-24:

> Have you given the horse strength? Have you clothed his neck with thunder?

> Can you frighten him like a locust? His majestic snorting strikes terror.

> He paws in the valley, and rejoices in his strength; he gallops into the clash of arms.

> He mocks at fear, and is not frightened; nor does he turn back from the sword.

> The quiver rattles against him, the glittering spear and javelin.

> He devours the distance with fierceness and rage;

> Nor does he come to a halt because the trumpet has sounded.

And in that moment, I knew what the promise was that I already had.

On that day at the Belmont Stakes, Secretariat's team of owner, trainer and jockey had decided to let this majestic horse run as fast as he wanted to go. It was a tremendous risk because race horses can outrun their physical capacity. The danger of running a horse to death is very real, but each one of them felt there was a greatness in Secretariat that had yet to be seen. So they chose to let him run—and history was made.

Years later, when Secretariat passed away, an autopsy was performed; and they discovered that his heart was twice the size of a normal horse's heart. It was completely healthy, but also enormous, something the experts present had never seen before. It was the answer to why Secretariat had been able to do the impossible.

And there it was, hidden in a story that God had likened my life to years ago and underscored with the verses from Job 39. It held my promise: my heart would not become restricted over time, but expansive in both the natural and the spirit. I would be able to not only finish my race but to do so in a manner that defied all reason.

It has become one of my Identity Statements, something I read aloud almost daily. "I am a warrior with the heart of a champion, created to overcome anywhere, anytime, under any conditions."

I've become good friends with my cardiologist since those early meetings. I look forward to seeing him occasionally so that I can work out on his treadmill, look over the reports, and wait for the words that have become familiar these past few years: "Everything looks great. I don't quite understand it, but nothing has changed."

Which is not quite true. While my physical heart remains stable, my heart as a champion has expanded exponentially. Such is the power of God's promises.

EPILOGUE

WHO DO YOU WANT TO BECOME?

That season of working with fine photography in Yosemite was a very long time ago in my life, over 30 years now. Back then, I didn't have a clue who God had created me to be, and I had a very distorted image of who He really was.

Through the years, there have been a number of encounters that have brought God's true identity and mine into clearer focus, but few have been as powerful as the heaven-to-earth perspective I gained in a maximum security prison. For over 15 years, I had the privilege of ministering in the enormous women's prisons of central California. God was always amazing, but the time that stands out most to me was when I inadvertently signed the team up to minister in the psychiatric cell blocks.

It happened when I sat down for a casual chat with Dave, our wonderful prison chaplain. I presented our team's request to visit the women on death row, but Chaplain Dave explained that the current rules wouldn't allow it—however, he desperately needed help in the same building working with those inmates who could no longer be in the general population because of their mental condition. I looked at this dedicated man, knowing his tireless work for the 4,000 women whom he was responsible for—and I said, "Okay." "Awesome!" Dave bounded up from his chair with a sincere and grateful smile. "You can start next Sunday . . . and thanks so much . . . really," and I knew he truly meant it. We were both behind schedule, so we said our quick good-byes and dashed out.

It was only after I was out of the building that it hit me. What in the world did I know about ministering to inmates with mental and emotional issues so significant that they had to be isolated from the population? The answer was . . . nothing. What I did know by now was the faithfulness of God when I was in over my head—and I was in *way* over my head.

So all week, I waited in expectancy. I anticipated that at any moment, God would say, "Teach this" or "Here's how to pray for them," but there was nothing—absolutely nothing. I could feel His peace and had a strong sense of His affection, but He was mute on the point of what to actually do on Sunday when the massive steel doors opened to Building 504.

By the time I began to check through security on Sunday, I still had no clue what this service would look like. It was over a quarter of a mile to Building 504, and there were several checkpoints that I had to pass through. At each one, I kept expecting God to say something, anything, but still not a sound—not until I passed through the last gate into the enormous processing yard where my destination lay at the far end.

As soon as I stepped onto that path, I was overwhelmed with the quiet, tangible sense of Jesus walking beside me. I was so thankful that I forgot to ask where He had been all week! I was just grateful that He was here now to tell me how to do this service—but what He did next was not at all what I was expecting.

It was as if my dear Friend was putting His hand gently on my shoulder. He quietly asked, "You know that teaching gift you have?" "Yes," I thought, expecting that He was about to give me the topic of today's service. "Well," His inner voice replied rather slowly, "I don't think you'll be needing that in here. How about if I hold on to that for you?" "Okay . . ." I responded hesitantly, "if You think that's best." "I do," He replied.

After another pause, He continued thoughtfully, "And you know that gift for worship that you have?" "Yes," I thought again, but added quickly, "You mean the one that You gave me?" "Yeah," said the Lord, "that's the one. How about if I hold on to that, too, for now?"

For as long as I had waited for God to deliver a plan, my sense of relief was quickly dissipating into panic. I could understand not doing some fancy teaching for these troubled inmates, but worship was kind of a no-brainer from my perspective. But I didn't have too long to think about that, because Jesus apparently had more items on His laundry list of things that He would like to "hold on to" for me. One by one, all the gifts that I felt I had gained during my life with Him were requested. As I could see myself passing each one into His hands, I began to feel more and more empty.

When I arrived at Building 504, I pushed the buzzer and stood still, quietly resigned to the fact that I had just relinquished everything I thought would prepare me for what lay on the other side of the massive door. It was at that moment that I felt His wonderful hand tap lightly on my chest, and I looked up into those immensely kind eyes. What Jesus said next forever transformed the image I had of God and of myself.

"Oh, and by the way—just remember, you have My heart. You're going to need that."

Suddenly, the doors clanged open and I was thrust into a dark, two story, concrete world of cell blocks and chaotic sounds. The officers were dressed in full riot gear and the signs on the walls warned of endless threats to my safety. A group of women was being led out— most with vacant eyes, many of them rocking back and forth as they were seated on the rows of benches. Above me, scores of women screamed and called out to the guards, angry that they weren't in the selected group below.

Once everyone found a place, the Holy Spirit whispered, "Sing 'Jesus Loves Me.'" And because I had absolutely no other idea of what to do—I did. While I have an acceptable voice, it was unlike anything I'd sung before. His passion joined with compassion for these dear ones and somehow entered into the words of the song so that it became a living and powerful truth. The room grew quieter; and when I finished, from somewhere in the back row, a thin, small voice ventured, "Sing it again . . . please."

In the years that have passed, I no longer remember how many times we repeated this process, but I believe it was in the range of about a dozen. When the song would end, another voice from a different part of the room would ask to hear it one more time. It was as if the Christ in me was singing directly to them, infusing every sound with how precious and priceless they were to Him.

I was overwhelmed by the power of Love as a person. It was no longer something God had. It was who He was.

Eventually, there were no further requests and I looked at the women before me. Their eyes were clear. Not one of them was rocking and many had tears rolling down their faces. I looked up to see the quiet faces of the women who had remained in their cells—silently joining with us. And behind the officer's desk, the guards stood absolutely still, many of them also in tears behind their face shields.

It was a moment when the atmosphere of heaven met earth. In that environment, women were physically healed, hearts were comforted, and lasting sanity was restored to many. For the next six months, our team was given incredible access to the most dangerous population in the prison. When we would ask the officers how long our visit should be that day, we often heard the reply, "Ladies, you can stay as long as you want to. It's the best day of our week for them— and for us."

What transformed me most about those months was realizing that the image I had of God was extraordinarily limited—and the image of myself and others was very earthbound. The miracles we saw that day and in the days that followed were not because of our magnificent gifts. It wasn't in our flashy teaching or understanding of how to minister to a crowd.

It was in beholding Him so profoundly, so intimately, that we had begun to become like Him. Paul said it beautifully in his letter to the Philippians. It is the truth that captures the essence of who I want to become in this life. For me, this excerpt from chapter 3, verse 10 from the Amplified Bible expresses it best: "That I may know Him— experientially, becoming more thoroughly acquainted with Him, understanding the remarkable wonders of His Person more completely."

Who do I want to be known as in this life? Who do I want to become? I want to behold the true Christ of the New Testament, not the one buried under old covenant legalism or modern political correctness. I want to travel with Him down unlikely roads, through unexpected experiences, into the deep valleys of comfort, and over the high places of His affection. Wherever He says to follow Him, that's where I want to go. On that journey, I want to behold who He really is: in the Bible, in worship, in the daily lives of my friends, and in my community. And in that process, to become an accurate reflection of Him in this life—so that when people encounter me, they get a taste of how good God really is and are able to see a bit of life on earth the way it is in heaven.

I profoundly believe that there are a growing number of people who are on that same journey. As with those first disciples, we are discovering that even though the distance between our present and God's intended future seems to be significant, it is the bridge of beholding and becoming that is closing the gap. As the true identity of the Father, Jesus, and Holy Spirit becomes clearer, our own is becoming more apparent. We relinquish our failing system of trying-harder-to-do-better for God and embrace the process of discovering just how loved we have always been. Our passion becomes filling up on the kindness and goodness of God and encountering the healing that His righteousness brings. How we think about God is the most important thought we'll ever have. Isn't it time to think as brilliantly about Him as He does about us?

Our truest identity will always be found in the intimate revelation of the heart and mind of Christ in us, our greatest hope of glory. Our identity begins with knowing who He really is—not just academically but experientially—and from that encounter, becoming an accurate, magnificent, unique expression of who He imagined us to be before we were ever born. Without that revelation, life becomes one dimensional and confusing. We become vulnerable to the lies of an enemy who seeks to steal our joy, our value and our very lives with his falsehoods of performance for acceptance and a warped image of a difficult-to-please God.

In Building 504, I encountered one of the darkest environments I had ever known—and Jesus shone the brightest. He didn't just bring them something through us; He brought Himself. Oddly enough, it wasn't until several months later that I realized I had never asked Him to return those gifts of mine that He was going to hold on to for me. Somehow, they had become more of a manifestation of His true identity and mine rather than something I possessed. I don't really understand how it works. I just know it's stayed that way.

There is an image of your life that God sees clearly, a masterpiece that most of the world has yet to understand, but it will revolutionize how they view the authentic followers of Christ. People both inside and outside the church are hungry for a breed of believers who know in whom they have believed and are fully confident of His ability to develop it fully in their lives and in the lives of others. People long to experience the truth of Zephaniah 3:17, "The Lord your God in your midst, The Mighty One, will save; He will rejoice over you with gladness, He will quiet you with His love, He will rejoice over you with singing." The Lord who is personally your God, the One who lives at the very core of who you are is continually celebrating your uniqueness with joy—singing the song of your life until you can sing it too.

The discovery of your truest identity isn't dependent on how gifted or smart or advantaged your life has or hasn't been. Whether the image of how God sees you is emerging or whether it still seems lost in a swirl of history and circumstances, the process is the same. The image of who you really are exists fully and completely in the heart of Father God and the brilliant mind of Christ, ready to be empowered by the Holy Spirit, your gracious personal Teacher, Helper and Comforter.

We are all in the process of seeing the image of ourselves that God already sees.

There is no obstacle so great that God cannot overcome it to produce the masterpiece of you that is His reality. It's a process that is not focused on who you have been, but only on who you are and who you are becoming.

It's a journey of the heart—from His to yours and from yours to others—an intimate and deeply personal revelation of who He really is to you and who you really are to Him that does not focus merely on changing behavior but on transformation into an accurate image of Christ and becoming everything He has envisioned in His eternal story of you.

PART 2

GUIDEBOOK: THE IMAGE

INTRODUCTION
TO THE IMAGE
GUIDEBOOK

The Image is a book that opens up the territory of identity in Christ. This guidebook is the GPS for actually entering in, navigating, and establishing it as your own experience. Just as we bring along a guidebook on a road trip that provides options of what to explore, where to eat, and what to see, this guidebook offers real world experiences with the truths you have been reading about and various possibilities of how you can pursue them.

The guidebook gives you the how without the how-to. There are no *10 Steps to a Better Identity* here; but instead, there's a host of interactive questions about who you really are in Christ. I didn't want to just tell you how you should perceive and think about your identity in God, but to actually give you ideas and tools that our Brilliant community[v] has discovered to be catalysts to personal transformation.

As you explore the questions included, it's good to remember—God rarely uses questions for the same reasons we do. Jesus did not present the good news in a standardized curriculum, nor is there a record of giving His disciples a pop quiz after He finished teaching: "The poor in spirit will . . . what? Anyone? Anyone?" In fact, Jesus asked scores of questions in the New Testament, and yet He only asked for answers on a handful of occasions. So why was He asking them?

God uses questions as catalysts for exploration. He is asking them to provoke our thinking, spark new understanding, and initiate a divine conversation. The "Questions for Exploration" connected with each chapter of the book are not to assess your comprehension of the material, but for you to make personal connections with what you've read and have a record of your process. They can be used again and again as you continue to grow in God, because your answers will expand or change as you do. And when you think of better questions than these, write those down and continue your exploration.

There is no lasting breakthrough without followthrough, but followthrough is not about memorizing facts or completing assignments. It's about relationally engaging with God because it is so delightful. The questions and tools are here for you to use in any way that works best for your unique personality, style of process and pace of development. God has handcrafted your experience with the material here, whether you explore this guidebook on your own, with a small group of friends or in a church setting.

After the questions that connect with each chapter of the book, there are activations and opportunities to look for clues to the image God has of you and tools to help you find the words to express it. There are too many to do all at once, so don't try to! Find a few that interest you and begin exploring. Some will fit your style better than others—so choose the ones that feel authentic to you. It's all part of God's discovery process as He walks with you and it's what differentiates a process from a program; and this is not a program, curriculum, or list of how-to instructions to be followed point by point.

It's a relational guide for your process of better understanding the image God sees when He looks at you—and a tangible tool for establishing your discoveries into your lifestyle with Him.

Exploring Chapters One through Six

You may have already read *The Image* from cover to cover—or maybe you have chosen to explore the questions as you read each chapter. Whatever works best for you is what you should do.

If you have already read the entire book, you may wish to read each chapter again before you dive into the questions. Your perspective has probably begun to change already, so you'll read things differently or discover ideas that may not have made a strong impression before.

When you're ready, enjoy interacting with the possibilities that these questions open up. Set aside any mindset of needing one right answer and needing it quickly. Think of this section as a form of journaling—a record of your story and journey into your true identity with the God who adores you.

YOUR LANDMARKS

There's a section for you to record a few key truths that you want to continue to investigate. These are like landmarks on the journey that you will want to explore more. Taking note of them is important because we can't process more than a handful of new or fresh perceptions at a time. You are certainly not limited to these, but they give you reference points for the future. You'll also find it highly rewarding to return to your initial notes a few weeks or months from now and realize how much you have been growing!

QUESTIONS FOR EXPLORATION

Use the "Questions for Exploration" as a compass to give you a sense of direction in how to unpack the primary truths of each chapter. Some questions are written to expand the material; others are created to connect with the relational aspects of processing God's truth. This is a great place to jot down any new questions you have.

QUESTIONS FOR GOD

"Questions for God" is a bit unique in that you are doing the asking not the answering. This may be a new experience for you. God adores questions, and He loves the divine conversation that they provoke. Simply write down what you feel He would say to the question you've asked. The Lord is filled with kindness, gentleness, and grace—His words will always be, too.

NEW THOUGHT

As we discussed in the "Upgrading Our Identity Software," we need to actively upgrade our perceptions and thinking as our understanding of God's true identity continues to mature. Our new revelations need to convert into new mindsets and language, or else our initial breakthroughs will begin to diminish into distant memories.

The "New Thought" section gives you the opportunity and space to find new words for the new way you want to think and speak about who you are. It's a place to practice your fresh perceptions and explore language you want to use when talking about your transforming image of God and who you are in Him.

ACTIVATING YOUR DISCOVERIES

Following the chapter explorations is a series of "activations." These describe a variety of ways in which to activate your learning. We're encouraged to not just be hearers but doers of the Word (James 1:22). It's great to read about the relational possibilities in discovering who God really is and who He created us to be—but unless we're equipped to make the relational journey, it's like reading a guidebook about Italy, Hawaii, or China, yet never going there. You can say that you know about those countries from reading about them, but you can't say that you've experienced them.

Spiritual development is always meant to partner knowledge with real-world encounters. Jesus didn't just give the disciples a teaching about miracles. He demonstrated them and then sent them out to practice. That's what activations are: practice opportunities. And the ones included here have creative tools for you to explore and expand.

All of them can be pursued on your own or in a small (or large) group of friends. If you are doing them yourself, you're creating a personal journal of your true identity as God sees it. If you are teaming together with others, you can use the questions to guide your discussion when you meet or answer them before you gather and share what you've discovered.

However you engage with this section of the book, remember that there is no set pace or prescribed timeline for completion. Allow yourself and any others you may be sharing this experience with to have a unique rhythm and approach. Expect a variety of responses because these are not questions with one prescribed answer. It's an exploration of new territory, so it's okay if you're not always sure of what comes next. It's why it's a guidebook not a workbook. Enjoy the adventure of it all.

OUR PRIMARY IDENTITY

YOUR LANDMARKS

What were a few new ideas or fresh perspectives that stood out to you in reading "Our Primary Identity"? Share the impact each thought has had on you so far:

QUESTIONS FOR EXPLORATION

Who or what do you feel has most influenced your image of God? List as many influences as you think have had impact.

Choose one aspect you have of God's image and describe it. What influenced your perception of this part of His image?

Describe a perception of God's image that you realize was probably not accurate in a sentence or two. What influenced your perception? How is it changing?

Think of an area in your life where you don't feel chosen. Imagine God standing next to you in that place. Slowly read Ephesians 1:3-6 aloud several times. Think about the meaning of the words. Feel the Father's great affection for you in them.

> Blessed be the God and Father of our Lord Jesus Christ, who has blessed us with every spiritual blessing in the heavenly places in Christ, just as He chose us in Him before the foundation of the world, that we should be holy and without blame before Him in love, having predestined us to adoption as sons by Jesus Christ to Himself, according to the good pleasure of His will, to the praise of the glory of His grace, by which He made us accepted in the Beloved. (Ephesians 1:3-6)

As He stands with you in that place where you haven't felt chosen or cherished, what would He say to you as His accepted one? Write it down here:

QUESTIONS FOR GOD

"Father, what do You see in me that I don't yet see in myself?" Write down what you think He would say to you:

NEW THOUGHT

Take this opportunity to have a new thought about yourself. How would you complete this statement? "When God looks at me, He sees . . ."

OVERCOMING OUR DEEPEST FEAR

YOUR LANDMARKS

What were a few powerful truths that impacted you in reading "Overcoming Our Deepest Fear," and why do you want to explore them more?

QUESTIONS FOR EXPLORATION

Think of an area in your life where you feel safer being small and unnoticed. Imagine that Jesus has slipped a note in your pocket to encourage you. What might it say?

What is one way that you feel God has created you to shine? (Share one here, but feel free to make a list of others!)

Where and how could you shine more brightly in this place?

What is preventing or limiting you from doing that?

Who does God want to be for you in overcoming that challenge? What is one aspect of His true nature that He wants to share with you that is bigger than any obstacle?

QUESTIONS FOR GOD

How do you think the Father might respond when you ask Him, "What is it about me as Your child that is well-pleasing to You?"

NEW THOUGHT

What is one way you would finish this statement: "I am one who shines brightly because . . ."

DOORS OF
OPPORTUNITY OR
OFFENSE

YOUR LANDMARKS

What thoughts surprised you or caught your attention while reading "Doors of Opportunity or Offense" that you want to explore further?

QUESTIONS FOR EXPLORATION

Think of a situation or person that you currently find challenging or frustrating. What negative emotions are you likely to experience?

How would you like to respond instead?

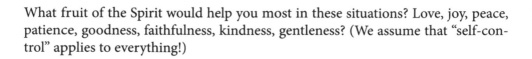

What fruit of the Spirit would help you most in these situations? Love, joy, peace, patience, goodness, faithfulness, kindness, gentleness? (We assume that "self-control" applies to everything!)

What are you looking forward to discovering about that fruit of the Spirit?

QUESTIONS FOR GOD

Think about the situation or person you are considering and ask, "God, when You look at this person or situation, what do You see?"

Look at the fruit of the Spirit that you chose and ask God, "Where do You see that fruit of the Spirit in my life now?"

NEW THOUGHT

What positive new thought might you add to the following sentence? "Under pressure, I am someone who responds with . . ."

Upgrading Our Identity Software

YOUR LANDMARKS

What were a few new ideas or fresh perspectives that stood out to you in reading "Upgrading Our Identity Software"? Share the impact each thought has had on you so far:

QUESTIONS FOR EXPLORATION

Activation #1

Fold a piece of paper vertically in half (creating two columns). On the left side, make a list of outdated or old mindsets about God that you realize you may be carrying around.

What is a better thought instead for each outdated mindset? Write that new thought on the right side across from the corresponding old mindset.

Choose one set of old and new mindsets about God that you would like to share:

Old mindset   New brilliant thought
about God   about His true nature

Activation #2

Now, get a second piece of paper and fold it the same way. On the left side, make a list of outdated or old mindsets about *yourself* that you may still be carrying around from your history.

And then on the right side, make a corresponding list of God's opposite thought for each old mindset. How does He see that area of your life in Christ? Who does He say you are? Choose one set of old and new mindsets about yourself that you would like to share:

Old mindset   New brilliant thought
about myself   about my true identity

Now read aloud only the new brilliant thoughts about God and yourself. What new freedoms do you think these thoughts will bring for you?

QUESTIONS FOR GOD

"Jesus, how does it make You feel to hear me say my new brilliant thoughts about You and about myself?" What do you think He might say?

"Holy Spirit, which one of these new brilliant thoughts about myself have You seen me reflect this week? Please remind me of how and where." Write down what comes to mind

NEW THOUGHT

How would you finish the following thought now: "Instead of seeing an old perspective of myself as . . . I am now seeing myself from God's perspective as . . ."

Freedom from Doing it All

What ideas or concepts in "Freedom from Doing It All" do you want to further explore? Jot a few notes by each on how you might do that:

QUESTIONS FOR EXPLORATION

What opportunities, jobs, or roles in life might be considered your Kingdom assignment(s)?

What do you enjoy most about each?

What is challenging about each?

Are there any Kingdom assignments you sense are yours that you haven't experienced yet? If so, what do you think they are?

QUESTIONS FOR GOD

"Father, are there any assignments on my list that are not on Yours?" Make a list of what you think these might be.

"Jesus, what actions have I taken this week that You will remember with a smile?" What comes to your mind?

NEW THOUGHT

Create a statement that expresses one of your Kingdom assignments: "I am one who thrives when I am . . ."

THE CURRENCY OF
IDENTITY

YOUR LANDMARKS

In "The Currency of Identity," what were some new thoughts or new perspectives on familiar truth that you discovered?

QUESTIONS FOR EXPLORATION

What is a promise in the Bible that you would like to take out as one of your gems? Write it out here:

What aspect of God's true nature do you see reflected in that promise?

What encouragement do you feel from that promise?

What obstacles in your life can this promise overcome?

QUESTIONS FOR GOD

What do you think God might say when you ask, "What is one way I'm created in Your image that I haven't discovered yet?"

And how might He answer the following? "What promises are You making to me that will help me become what You already see in me?"

NEW THOUGHT

What is one way that you would finish this statement? "God has promised me that I am and am becoming . . ."

Introduction to
Identity Clues

Creating an Identity Statement
and Evidences of Transformation

So now you've finished reading the chapters filled with fresh mindsets about who God really is and who He created you to truly be. You have spent time considering "Questions for Exploration" and a dialogue is developing between you and the Lord —and possibly a few of your friends.

The way you perceive and think about identity may
be shifting, but the process is actually just beginning.

Behavioral change without the spiritual transformation of our perceptions, mindsets, language and actions is largely based on self-effort and raw discipline. It can occur, but joy and longevity are usually not sustainable.

As we begin to see more of the true nature of God, how we see ourselves begins to transform. Our perceptions and mindsets begin to reflect how the mind of Christ perceives and thinks. Our language and actions are the next outward evidences that transformation is occurring. Because we are perceiving and thinking more accurately about God and ourselves, how we speak and what we choose to do begins to change—and you want to have a way to record that transformation so that you can continue to connect the dots of your development and be encouraged by the upgrades that are occurring in your life!

Transformation is fueled by joyful intentionality, because now we're not just thinking about God's story of us; we're embracing our central role in it! We are rejoicing in our breakthroughs, but we are also actively looking to follow through in a way that will establish the truths we are discovering. Our true identity in Christ is no longer just a concept that we hope to one day understand. We're partnering with God in seeing His reality become ours.

This part of the guidebook for *The Image* is a rich resource of ways you can explore who God created you to be and ideas for a continued divine conversation. These resources are some of the ways I've discovered in traveling through the territory of our identity in Christ.

**There are a lot of creative ideas here, so pace
yourself. They are not all meant to be done at once or
to be done quickly.**

Enjoy looking them over, and then choose one that you would like to explore first. These ideas are ways to gather further clues about who God created you to be. They are not academic exercises, but more like tools in a tool room. Enter in, look around, and then choose a starting point. Find one that intrigues you and use it for a while. Jot some notes down; explore as long as you're interested; and then choose another area and go exploring there. The Identity Clues don't necessarily need to be done in order. All of them can be done individually or in a group, and there are adaptations that are listed.

When you're interested, try writing down a few statements of identity that you can read aloud and begin to say, "Yes, this is the image that God sees when He looks at me." Utilize the section that gives you more ideas about actually writing and working with an Identity Statement.

And then at various times in your journey, consider the Evidences of Transformation that you've encountered, and write them down using the guide provided here. Spiritual development cannot be assessed by a test of comprehension of the material. It is found in the real-life stories in which you identify how your perceptions, mindsets, language, and actions are changing. It's when you discover that you're responding to your circumstances, other people, and your own behavior in a completely new way! You can use this tool again and again as you continue to explore God's true identity and yours.

No matter which part of this section of the book you engage with, keep it fun, joyful, and adventurous. That's the nature of God toward you on this exploration, and it delights Him to see you approach it the same way.

Identity Clues - Inheritance Words

"Where do I begin to look for the image God has of me and who He created me to be?" It's one of the questions I'm asked the most. There's no one definitive answer or specific place to start, because then it would be a program to follow, not a relational process with God to be explored. But here are some good possibilities that some of us on this journey have found to be helpful.

A wonderful starting place is what we call Inheritance Words in our Brilliant community. These are the scriptures that leap off of the page and captivate our heart. They can become evident while we're reading the Bible, in an encouragement given by a friend, or spoken to our heart. However we receive them, Inheritance Words seem to take on a life of their own and become places of comfort and deep wells of life to go to when we're hurting and that encourage us again and again. In them you will find a three-dimensional picture of the authentic nature of God, but they also hold clues to who you are as well.

My earliest inheritance word was Joshua 1:9: "Only be strong and very courageous, for the Lord thy God is with you, whithersoever thou goest" (KJV). I can still only think of it in the old King James language, hearing my mother read it to me as an eight-year-old child because I was terrified of everything. There was something in the cadence of those ancient words that gave me such peace and hope. She told me the stories of Joshua, both of his triumphs and his failures. He wasn't a distant figure to me because of that. His story was living and real, one that I've discovered a great deal of myself in.

Look at the scriptures and the people in the Bible whom you consider friends, heroes of the faith who continue to cheer you on today. What do they say about who you are? What promises are there for you to explore and mine deeply?

**Joyfully ask God for inheritance words. It's a
prayer He loves to answer, though His answers may
surprise you.**

When I knew I was to leave my twenty-year teaching career to embark on an entirely new life creating developmental spiritual communities with Graham Cooke, I was truly walking off my map of security, competency, and a long family tradition of having one career in a lifetime. It was exciting and overwhelming, wonderful and weird.

I knew I would need a good, solid compass for the journey ahead, and I began to ask God for a new Inheritance Word for this transition. I expected verses about adventure, courage, or taking risks, maybe a passage about being an overcomer and champion. But He had a different idea. Instead of fueling my excitement, the Holy Spirit went straight after my identity as His beloved one by whispering words from Psalm 139. He chose to focus on how loved I have always been by God, how intricately He knows my life, and how deeply He cares. It was His promise that this journey would be filled with His infinite good thoughts toward me and His complete understanding of who He created me to be.

It seemed an odd choice for an emerging warrior, but oh my goodness, how this passage of Scripture has been my safe place in ways I couldn't have possibly imagined! God's wisdom to make this transition about who we were together, rather than the job or battle at hand, was both genius and extraordinarily necessary in the years ahead. Psalm 139 is a tangible place in my spirit, the true high tower of His affection that I can hide and abide in. The words are new and fresh to me every time I read them.

So ask and keep on asking when it comes to inheritance words. Once you discover one, stay with it for weeks, even months. Make those words the focus of your devotion, worship, and meditation; and they will continue to open up to you. Scripture holds great treasures showing us how our identity can become as evident on earth as it is in heaven.[vi]

EXPLORING INHERITANCE WORDS FOR IDENTITY

1. Make a list of key scriptures that have been pivotal in your life with God or you would consider your inheritance words.

2. Take one of these scriptures and find a quiet place. Read it aloud several times. Think of how it has encouraged you and the circumstances in your life when it did so. What are the feelings that rise up when you read these words? Write those thoughts down.

3. What are you most thankful for in these verses? Write a note to God about that. "Father, thank You that . . ."

4. Are there any promises that God is making to you in this passage? If so, what are they? These are part of your rich inheritance to be found here.

5. What aspect of God's true nature do these verses reflect?

6. What is the image God has of you that are reflected in these scriptures? Write these out as if God were saying them directly to you. "I see you as . . ." Read it aloud daily and soak in His words of affirmation and assurance.

Consider staying with this one passage of Scripture for several weeks or months—not reading anything else during this time. It may be challenging at first, but deep truth takes time to unfold. Continue to take notes about what God shows you in them regarding His true nature and the image He sees when He looks at you.

(For more on Inheritance Words, you may wish to explore "Identity and Inheritance" CDs/MP3s by Graham Cooke. And the *Joyful Intentionality* chapter entitled "But I Don't Have a Prophetic Word" by Allison Bown. Both are available at www.BrilliantBookHouse.com.)

Identity Clues - God's Words to You

Friends adore talking to friends. God has given us so many wonderful gifts, and hearing His voice is one of our promises from Him (John 10:3-4). God talks to us through our times of devotion and worship, and through words of encouragement, comfort, and exhortation from His friends with a gift that we call prophetic ministry (1 Corinthians 14:3-5).

For those who have had access to quality prophetic ministry, you may have received prophetic prayer or words of prophecy. If you have a recording or notes on these, pull them out and look for descriptions of your identity as God sees you. Prophetic words can be studied and examined, which is one way to unpack them. But they can also be processed relationally by considering their impact on who God is to you and what He is saying about who He created you to be.

Good prophetic training teaches us to actively work with our words, connecting them with scriptures, finding common themes and highlighting key phrases. This is an enormously helpful, valid and powerful part of purposefully engaging with the words we've received. As the Holy Spirit commented to me many years ago regarding my prophetic words, "They're not baseball cards to be collected. Kindly use them."

Some people have found it very helpful to transcribe their words in bullet points for study, leaving lots of room and space to make notes. Then consider these brilliant questions, adapted from Graham Cooke's Schools of Prophecy:

- What are key words or phrases that are repeated or make a strong impression?

- Are there scriptures in the prophetic word? If so, list those.

- Are there other scriptures not mentioned but that you want to add?

- What are specific descriptive words that are used? Make a list.

- Are there themes that appear throughout the word? Group those thoughts together.

- What are the promises that this word contains?

- Are there any conditions required of you that are stated?

But there is also a relational aspect to interacting with quality prophetic words. For this, it can be helpful to write out your prophetic word as if it were a letter from God to you in a manner that you can easily read aloud. This gives you a version to use as a devotional copy during times of meditation.

Spend time thinking deeply about the sound of the Father's voice, as if He were saying this word directly to you. If the word was given to you verbally, hopefully it was by someone who was able to capture God's heart in its delivery; but if that was not the case, you can still discover the tone of His voice in it. Would He say it warmly, with great affection? Or maybe with empowering strength that communicates His passionate protection. Did He want to express it in a manner that imparted peace and hope to you? Ask the Holy Spirit to show you and consider the tone of the word the way He intended it.

In engaging with prophetic words relationally, we simply enjoy listening and receiving from the God who adores us. Allow thanksgiving to rise in your heart and bubble up with encouragement and joy. You might want to read the devotional version of your word aloud as part of your times of personal worship. If a particular phrase captivates your heart, stay with it for a while. Don't take notes. Just continue to think deeply about that phrase or a scripture that you're connecting with.

The world's version of meditation is to empty our minds. God's perspective on meditation is that we fill up on His good thoughts and plans for us, on His promises and on His words of new life, so that there simply isn't any more room for negativity, fear, doubt or unbelief.

Once you've taken these preliminary steps and soaked in the joy of your prophetic words or comfort (1 Corinthians 14:3), consider some of these relational questions on a separate paper. In fact, I highly recommend creating a three-ring notebook with sections for each of your prophetic words with your responses to the following questions.

Use the following questions as a guide to dig deeper into your words:

- What does this word say about who God wants to be for you?

- Is that how you have perceived Him or is there an upgrade for your perceptions here?

- If an upgrade is needed, what is the old perception you have had, and what is the new truth that displaces it?

- What kind of person does this word describe you to be? Create a character description.

- What aspects of that character description do you feel are currently evident in your life?

- What are areas of further growth and development you will need in order to become the kind of person described?

- What is the gap between who you are now and who you could become in the fullness of this word? What are the missing pieces, and how does God want to provide them?

Often times in prophetic ministry, we focus on what the word says we will be doing rather than who we will become in the process. Always pay the most attention to *who* the word talks about you being and who God desires to be for you.

Any actions that the prophetic word also includes must be the result of an upgraded relationship with God first so that you are well-equipped for the fulfillment of your word. Does the word require practical training in skills you don't currently have? Talk to God about how best to pursue those. It's not about conspiring to make your prophetic word happen but relationally partnering with God in the process of the development it requires. Personal prophetic words speak to our potential, not our inevitable.

The key question of identity with any prophetic word is, who will you need to become to inherit the fullness of those words?

Enjoy exploring your prophetic word both intentionally and relationally: study them intentionally to mine out the treasures of truth; and engage with them relationally to encounter who God wants to be for you and who you are becoming.

However you choose to explore your prophetic words, keep the central themes of identity in focus: what are you seeing about God's true nature, and what is revealed about how He sees you?

And one last note: if you haven't had access to personal prophetic ministry, check out a corporate prophetic word.[vii] There's a list of possibilities in the resource section at the end of this book. You can also use the same questions above for a corporate prophetic word just as well as a personal one. It will be your own conversations with the Holy Spirit that will take these from a general prophetic word to your personal word from the Lord.

Identity Clues – The Power of Pictures

The foundation of these activations are based on my early experiences in Graham's workshops many years ago. Since then, I've created several variations of the original activation that I've used in many places to facilitate dialogue about our Kingdom identity. We've done them with groups ranging from 200 people to a small gathering of three or four friends. And often, I do it with the Holy Spirit by myself just because it's fun. It's looking and responding to pictures and images and considering what they communicate about God's perspective on who we are to Him.

There's a reason "a picture says a 1,000, words." Imagery contains layers that often transcend spoken language. Consider pictures you are captivated by. Remember how this book started? It was with a photograph that had done just that. God could be using an image to communicate a spiritual truth, as well as a marker that points to a greater understanding of who He created us to be.

All of these activations begin with extended worship and rejoicing that create an atmosphere that reflects the delight God has in us. At my conferences or workshops, there are usually several teaching sessions about identity, most of which are covered in the first section of this book. After saturating ourselves in the image God sees when He looks at our lives, it's time to creatively interact with the truths we've been exploring.

ACTIVATION #1 - SMALL GROUP

The original activation is to take a collection of pictures and turn them face down on the floor or table. People are asked to get into groups of three (preferably with people they don't know well—but that's not required), and then each take a turn getting a picture and picking it up in a way that they don't see what it is. I suggest having people turn it toward their chest. Once seated, the person with the picture turns it around so that others can see it but they can't.

The objective is for the two other people in the group to look at the image, rest in stillness, and consider what God might say about how He sees the person holding the photograph. I always ask those who can see the picture to not say anything initially, but take time to soak in the image. After your first impression, what are the details you see—and most of all, what do they mean for this person? There's a difference between giving a description of an image and interacting with the Holy Spirit as to what it means. That's what we encourage people to go for, but don't overthink it. After a couple of minutes of quiet, I gently ask one of the people not holding the picture to begin to share what they feel they are seeing from God's perspective.

When I first did this, there were no such thing as smart phones, and people rarely carried recorders with them. So one of the two people without a picture took notes and the other spoke about it for a minute or two. Then, they traded places. The person who had been taking notes became the speaker, and the other became the note taker. Of course, it can still work that way, but most people just turn their phones on to record what is said.

Before we begin, we always pray together with joy and expectation. We anticipate that God has good things to say to His beloved ones. As I mentioned, I learned this as a way to activate the prophetic gift—however, I've used it in places that probably couldn't even spell prophetic (or would have chosen not to) and had the same results. When you first create an atmosphere of God's passion for people and His loving kindness toward them, and then ask people to simply express what He would say to the person before them through this picture, the Holy Spirit tends to take over from there.

All of my pictures from old magazines, greeting cards, and the internet are positive images that I've had a delightful time collecting with the Lord. You would have to work pretty hard to say something negative to a person based on these pictures, but just in case, I have a very, very simple instruction: "Be Nice." We're working in the territory of 1 Corinthians 14—speak words of edification, encouragement, and comfort.

I never cease to be astounded at what happens next. Many people are not used to sitting and hearing God's words of affirmation pour over them. The stories are endless of people using specific language that has personal meaning for the listener. Participants range from deeply encouraged to powerfully impacted by the words they hear.

I once watched an older woman get a bit flowery and lengthy in sharing what she saw in the picture. The young teenager waiting to speak seemed to wilt in her chair the longer the "experienced" minister-type woman went on. You could see her thoughts written on her face: "How am I going to follow that?" The receiver seemed to be listening politely but not particularly connecting. (Though you can't always go by that, as everyone has a very different posture and personality in receiving.)

I wasn't close enough to hear what the young girl said when it was finally her turn, but God bless her, she was brave enough to say something. It was pretty much just one whispered sentence, muttered tentatively—but it was straight from the Father's heart. The face of the woman who was receiving simply melted into the most beautiful smile, and tears of joy and relief began to flood down her cheeks. From what I remember, the girl had used an exact phrase that God had already spoken to this woman's heart—a promise that had become almost too impossible to believe in her current circumstances. It was a powerful affirmation for her that she had heard Him accurately and that He loved her enough to be sure she knew that He hadn't forgotten.

One sentence spoken with compassion and grace can change everything for someone—so always give what you have. If Jesus can feed 5,000-plus people with one lunch of loaves and fishes, He can take your words and expand their impact exponentially. Less is often more.

It's only after each person has spoken that the receiver gets to see their picture. This is where smart phones are not only good as a recording device but as a camera.

In the "old days," I lost a lot of pictures to people who simply couldn't part with theirs. Now they can take a photo of their picture, and I don't have to continually go hunting for new ones. I always encourage people to keep looking, writing, and processing. This activation is really just a starting point for you and the Holy Spirit to continue your conversation about your true identity.

ACTIVATION #2 - GOD'S WORDS OF LIFE TO YOU

This activation can be done in a group, but it works just as well to do it on your own. All you have to do is choose a photograph or image you are drawn to. Everything else remains the same.

In this variation, I turn all of the pictures face up and encourage people that the instructions are very simple this time: just come get a picture you love. If I don't have enough photographs for everyone, then more than one person can share a picture or take a picture of it with their phone to work from. Once that's done, I ask them to return to their seats or find a place to sit and write.

Once the room is settled, there's usually anticipation for who they are going to share an encouragement with this time based on the picture they chose. And that's where the Holy Spirit sneaks up on them. I simply say, "The picture is for you. What is the Father saying about how He sees *you* through that image? Write it down. And the same rules apply: Be nice."

Most people are far more used to saying positive things to others than they are about themselves. It can be easier to speak about God's goodness, grace, and kindness to strangers than it is to believe that He feels that way around them, too, much less take the time to write it down. If people are sharing a picture, I remind them not to talk about it but simply write.

The previous group activation has gotten them into the flow of seeing God's heart in the pictures; this one tends to open a flood gate for a divine conversation. I have emails and letters from people who have continued to collect pictures and have sat in stillness to hear the Father speak His kind words over them. Some have made photo albums or bulletin boards of their favorite pictures and added scriptures; and recently, one friend decoupaged a coffee table with them! It's really beautiful—not to mention a pretty great conversation starter at a party.

ACTIVATION #3 - PICTURES IN YOUR LIVING SPACES

My house is filled with pictures, paintings, and images that bring me joy. Some are from my days working with photographers who are dear friends; others are paintings by my father. I have relics from battlefields and sculptures of bronze that inspire me. You'll also see a great deal of handcrafted work, from pottery to baskets to a magnificent hardwood dining table that I designed and my master carpenter husband built. I highly value unique pieces with a story.

Recently, I hung a multi-media piece in my office that is quite different than the other artwork in my home. It is a abstract painting called "The Creation." My mother and I discovered it while roaming an art festival in Southern California one weekend. It's a three-dimensional collage of paint, paper, and iridescent strands that we both adored. I've been enjoying it all over again as I consider the next adventures ahead of me that currently feel rather unformed but still highly anticipated. It's unique, undefined, and colorful—which is a pretty excellent description of a key part of my persona in this current season.

Consider the photographs, artwork, and images that you've surrounded yourself with in your daily life. What do they say about who you are? Art is highly subjective. It's quite possible that the reason you connected with these pieces enough to display them holds another clue to who God made you to be.

Enjoy gaining new lenses to see the imagery around your life. Engage in actively exploring what God might have to say through them, and take notes on the clues to identity which they may hold for you.

Identity Clues - Who Are Your Heroes?

"Every culture has its icons—legends who become larger than life as their story is told and retold. In days past, these heroes have often been war and political figures whose images are burned in our mind's eye . . . As the Western world has evolved, we have seen our cultural heroes shift from revolutionary warriors to sports figures and entertainers . . .

But these icons pale in comparison to the influence of spiritual heroes. The lives of these war heroes and entertainment superstars have been examined and chronicled, but never to the degree of the heroes of the Bible . . . for centuries people have looked to the lives of these spiritual heroes for guidance and inspiration. How did they do it?

How did someone like that change the world?"[viii] Graham Cooke ~ *Qualities of a Spiritual Warrior*

All of us have heroes in our lives or people who we greatly admire because of the impact they have had. For some, it is a valiant single mother, an older brother, or a caring grandparent. Others have had teachers who made a difference or coaches who taught them more than just the rules of sport. Many of us have been blessed to have exceptional mentors and wonderful fellow travelers on this journey who inspire us to become more than we thought we could be.

There are people in history who capture our imagination, and their courage reminds us of what is possible for those who are passionately committed to a just cause. And there are those in the Bible who become more than characters in a distant story—they become overcomers and champions whose lives have personally impacted our own.

HEROES AND IDENTITY: PART 1

Who are you inspired by? Jot down a name or two for each of the categories below. The people you list from history, your community, or your family do not have to necessarily be Christians but simply have something about their character that has inspired you.

- Bible:
- History:
- Family:
- Christians alive today (whom you may or may not know personally):
- People from any other personal experience, such as a workplace, school, or community:

Now for each person you listed, consider the primary character attribute that resonates strongly with you. Most people will have several, but for the purposes of this activation, choose one. Write that single word or phrase next to each name.

After you have finished that, take each of these descriptive words you used and simply make a list of the character attributes that you've chosen.

When you've finished, turn the page to continue on to the next section. This is not a test or quiz. The answers are uniquely yours, so I encourage you not to peek at what we will do next with this list—but of course that's totally up to you.

HEROES AND IDENTITY: PART 2

How does this list of personal heroes apply to your exploration of identity?

**The list of character attributes you see in your heroes
or in those you greatly admire often reflect who God
created you to be.**

Just as a magnet is attracted to metal, our hearts are often inspired by attributes of character that reflect our own identity. They stir a dream in our hearts of who we desire to be, too.

Maybe that has been your experience—and maybe it hasn't. Any activation is really a matter of exploration and possibilities to see what fits best for you. But spend time with the list you have made and consider what might be hidden in your heroes that reveals a fresh perspective about who God created you to be.

Someone who had recently heard my teaching sessions on identity with this activation sent me a great example of what I've seen happen many times in my travels:

> The first hero I thought of was Anne Sullivan, Helen Keller's teacher. Scenes from the movie *The Miracle Worker* came to mind, and I found it online and watched it. I had first seen it when I was nine years old, and even then I had been deeply impacted by how she had been able to reach Helen when no one else could.
>
> I remember the impact of the statement at the end of the activation: "Those heroes and the primary quality that you admire in them . . . It's you! You're probably drawn to the excellence in them because it's part of your DNA too."
>
> So I thought about Anne Sullivan, who had lost much of her sight at a young age and, because of this, refused to give up on Helen when someone else might have. I could really identify with her passion for others to experience freedom and goodness, because for many years as a Christian, I was in bondage to religion and performance.
>
> Then about ten years ago, I discovered how good the Father was and understood His passion and love for me. I became passionate about sharing it so that others could experience the same kind of breakthrough and joy.

So the Identity Statement that grew from this hero is, "I am called to release and proclaim the goodness of God and to draw His sons and daughters into intimacy with their heavenly Father."

The image that God sees of us is often revealed piece by piece. If there are pieces of your identity to be discovered in those you would consider heroes or in people you greatly admire, enjoy the exploration and the conversation with God as to the attributes in them that He may well have deposited in you, too.

Identity Clues - Ideas from Fellow Travelers

People are amazingly creative because we have a creative God. I've always enjoyed hearing how one idea sparks another and how people expand on the basic ideas given to them. Many of my fellow travelers on this journey have shared unique ways that they have embarked on this identity discovery. Enjoy these examples from their explorations, and see if there are a few here that you connect with. They can serve as creative discussion starters you can expand on with the Holy Spirit and your friends.

- Pay attention to key phrases and common themes you receive from Scripture or encouragement from others. For several months, my friend Teresa continuously heard, "You're covered!" It became a statement of her identity, perfect for pulling out in tenuous circumstances.

- Heart's desires and passions. What do you love to do? I have a friend who is a great photographer, but he's also someone who excels in seeing beauty in people that others might miss or underestimate. And he's a genius at knowing how to draw it out for others to see, too. His identity is reflected in why he loves photography.

- What makes you angry? Are you mad when you see injustice or abandoned children? Does wastefulness of resources or the condition of poor neighborhoods make you see red? There are some good clues in there as to what God has raised you up to fight and overcome. Moses' passion against injustice was misdirected in his early life (Exodus 2:14), but it was an authentic part of who he was.

- Music that connects with you deeply. What songs have become the soundtrack for your life, and what are the lyrics that resonate most with you? Maybe there's something there to explore?

- Interests or courses of studies pursued. There's a great story of a team member who majored in exercise physiology but never really pursued it as a career. One day she realized that she was a natural trainer in the ways of God. One of her key Identity Statements is, "I am a personal trainer to the Body of Christ" and then she expands on how she spiritually creates exercises that strengthen others in their relationship with God.

- Movies you are passionate about. I adore the scene in *Apollo 13* where the NASA Director says, "This could be the worst disaster NASA's ever experienced." And Gene Kranz, the legendary chief of Mission Control, responds immediately, calmly, and decisively—"With all due respect, sir, I believe this is gonna be our finest hour."[ix] He was not going to stand by and foster an atmosphere of negativity and fear at this most critical juncture. I can't tell you how deeply that's who I am and desire to be.

- Who we are may also be reflected in positive childhood nicknames. One of mine was "Spee" for "spelunker," because I was always curious and adventuresome, just like a cave explorer. That's certainly a part of who I am! Another friend was called "Pooh Girl" for her love of Winnie-the-Pooh, a character that she shares a lot of qualities with. She has thought about what those specific qualities are, and they have become part of who she knows God sees her as.

- Pay attention to night dreams—where you have experiences that point to your identity in ways you might miss when you're awake.

- What does your personal history reflect of who you really are? I remember the story of a lovely woman who shared how God connected a childhood movie with an incident she heard about long after it occurred. She had always loved Snow White, especially when the prince brought her back to life. Years later, she was told the story of her birth. After three days, her mother's active labor stopped, and she was scheduled for a C-section the following morning to remove the stillborn fetus. A group of dear women prayed all night long; and the following day, everyone was shocked when the baby cried loudly after being removed! She really was Snow White coming back to life and has explored what God has hidden in that story for her.

- Asking for observations from teachers, mentors, or people who have worked with you can be hugely helpful. My pal Eric surveyed different mentors he had partnered with over the years and asked them to list the three greatest qualities that they had observed in him. When he got the responses, he saw the patterns and asked the Holy Spirit to show him connections from His perspective.

- Review old journals or letters for the positive attributes they reflect. Is there a common strand that you see in them that you have never connected about your true passions and identity? A good friend remarked that reviewing old journals with this lens was like a treasure hunt, filled with riches. She also discovered that there were a lot of old mindsets and junk, too. She decided to collect the treasure and then discard the rest. What a great idea.

- Pay attention to repeated observations by friends, co-workers, and family. If there are a number of people in your life who continually say, "You're really good at writing," or "The way you write helps me understand it better," take note of those.

- Some people develop standard questions that they use to assess possible identity clues. I particularly like these that were shared with me:

  1. To what or whom am I drawn as to a magnet?

  2. To what degree (and for how long) has this drawing or desire dominated my thoughts and actions?

  3. What is distinctive about my approach or abilities in the area(s) to which I'm intensely drawn or in which I receive strong affirmation?

  4. What opportunities for development continually evoke a "Yes!" in me?

  5. What exists in me that I cannot live without being or doing?

- Observe the opposites of what have previously been obstacles or areas of warfare. The key question here is, "What is the enemy so afraid of about who I am that he must oppose it?" This can be a very significant way to discover key pieces of your true identity and deserves a couple of great examples.

In a very acrimonious situation, a longtime friend realized that God had placed her there as an "Ambassador of God's love." Instead of letting this phrase drift away after the situation was resolved, she held on to it—exploring what it meant to be an ambassador and how it manifested in situations like the one she had just experienced. By observing how God mobilized her on earth, the phrase became a key that opened up a significant understanding of how she is known in heaven,

Another friend of mine shared, "I took the 'opposite' approach too. I looked at what had been my biggest insecurities and hardest obstacles in life and asked what the opposite of these were. In them, the Father revealed some of my best attributes. For example, I had struggled with feelings of not being smart my whole life, and yet the Lord continued to put me in the path of insanely smart people. In fact, five out of the seven kids I've helped raise are geniuses!

I asked the Lord one day why he kept putting these genius kids in my life when I felt so unfit to guide them. The Father said, "I need you to understand how a genius' mind works, because I have made you a genius in the spirit—learning quickly, grasping information, and moving at an accelerated pace." After that, I never looked at my shortcomings or insecurities the same again. Now I know how to look for God's opposite instead and how He perceives what I saw as lack.

Wherever God prompts you to look, explore or think deeply, keep your process joyful and light. God can only communicate in the language of the fruit of the Spirit, so His words to you will always be filled with love, joy, peace, patience, kindness, goodness, and gentleness.

Sort through all the ideas you've read here so far and choose *one* from this or preceding chapters to focus on and start with.

Resist negativity and find God's opposites for any that emerge.

Be gracious with yourself in this process, tuning your spiritual ears to hear His delight in your journey.

For Him, it's not about how fast you do or don't get it. The Father, Jesus, and the Holy Spirit are just so happy that you're digging deeper into who they created you to be.

Consider ideas found in this book simply as a springboard for what you can create and develop next.

CREATING, WRITING AND USING IDENTITY STATEMENTS

So you've gone exploring who God created you to be and have gathered some identity clues and upgraded your mindsets. What comes next?

At some point, it is a good idea to begin to capture a few statements in words that you can read, revise, adapt, and meditate on. The creation of an Identity Statement isn't like some type of doctoral thesis. It is not something that you will do once and then frame on the wall. It's meant to be a living document that grows as you do. So if there is any sense of needing to get it right before you are willing to start, let it go now. This is about continuing to gain more clarity regarding the image of you that God sees, nothing more than that. And if you miss an element or don't use the best words possible, it's not as if your true identity no longer exists! You can change your Identity Statement as often as you like.

YOU ALREADY HAVE SOME

Go back and look at what you recorded under each "New Thought" section found at the end of each of the six chapters you explored in this book. Each "New Thought" is actually a statement of identity! Sneaky, huh?

I've learned over time that people often perceive the act of beginning an Identity Statement as a much bigger challenge than it needs to be, so these give you a running start. Write them out on a single piece of paper or use small index cards for each one and toss them into the pile of possibilities.

BEGIN BY COLLECTING

This process begins by collecting, not sorting. You don't have to decide how the pieces and clues you gather are meant to fit together yet. And most of all, don't try to cram in everything from *The Image* and the questions here. Remember, the book is a resource, meant to be worked with over weeks, months, and years.

One incredibly practical way I begin this process is by simply having a box where I can record and toss in my identity clues. Whether it's a picture, a scripture, or a note on something I've discovered, I don't try to initially figure out where it connects. This keeps everything together so that I don't lose key pieces, but it also allows me the time for processing and considering before I try to put words to them. Some people have used pockets in a notebook, but the main feature is to see yourself initially as a collector, not a connector.

JUMP RIGHT IN

When you do want to begin to articulate your identity, remember that you only need to begin with a few statements. Remind yourself that you can change and update it as many times as you like, so you don't have to wait to have a perfect statement fully formed before writing it down. Just the act of jumping in will open up the process for you—so dive in!

If you've gathered a lot of pieces and aren't sure where to start, the answer is "anywhere you want to!" Write a statement down, and you're on your way.

You may want to begin with a time of worship and focus on the One who loves you best. Read Psalm 139 aloud, and consider God's endless good thoughts of you, the ones that outnumber the sands of the sea. Spread out a few of the ideas about your identity that you may have collected so far and allow a sense of anticipation to rise. There are some treasures here! Engage actively with the Holy Spirit as your Teacher and Helper, declaring your confidence in Him to be true to His identity for you in this process. Keep it joyful, fun, relational, and delightful.

ARROWS TO THE TARGET

Initially, you just want to write some basic statements down; but over time, begin to refine the language to become concise, sharp, and easy to remember. This is especially true if you are working from scriptures or prophetic words that may contain poetic language. Skip the flowery images and go for the meaning behind them.

The Identity Statement that came from my Secretariat promise is a good example: "I am a warrior with the heart of a champion, created to overcome anywhere, anytime, under any conditions." Notice that there's nothing about a horse in that statement.

A lengthy poetic version of this might be: "I am a Secretariat, a grand champion race horse that can overcome adversity and win any race because God created me with a heart that is bigger and stronger and has placed me with a team that will always let me run to my full capacity." The reality is, I'm not a racehorse; I'm a human being. It's the *meaning* of the story that speaks to my identity.

Write in everyday language. Resist "Christianese" whenever possible because it isn't spoken by most of the world. It's wise to avoid an Identity Statement as such, "I am a blessed and highly favored child of the most high King, sanctified for His purposes, surrounded by a hedge of protection, and covered by the blood of Jesus." Okay, please hear this next sentence with all the kindness in the world: to someone who doesn't know Jesus yet, this kind of sounds like you got lost in the royal gardens at Buckingham Palace after a rather vicious assault had taken place. If you were raised in church, you may well have been immersed in this vocabulary; but for an Identity Statement, it's best to speak in normal language. Go more for something like, "I am a beloved daughter of Jesus the King, walking in the fullness of His favor, protection, and righteousness."

The other reason for concise, everyday language is that you want a statement that you can remember under pressure. My favorite Identity Statement for the relationships in my life has only nine words: "I am a faithful friend of a Faithful Friend."

Start as expansively as you need to just to get words to paper. But then refine your statement to reflect the meaning behind the sources that you've drawn from, and create a declaration that you can remember easily so that it becomes a powerful part of your spiritual arsenal when the enemy tries to tell you differently.

INCLUDE PRESENT AND FUTURE

Identity Statements are not only about who you are but also who you are becoming. You want to have a variety of statements that not only reflect your present but also your future. If all of your statements are ones that are fully realized in your life today, then you probably want to explore some that speak to the potential God sees in you as well.

On the other hand, if your statements are so futuristic that a close friend listening to them wouldn't be able to tell who it was about, you might want to dial it back a bit from the intergalactic ministry range into something that is more relevant to your daily life.

A great tool that was suggested for this is to create a scale to evaluate your statements. I use a 1, 2 or 3 to indicate how much the statement is part of my current reality: 1 means very present; 2 means emerging; 3 means just becoming evident. Another friend of mine uses a five-point scale; another has a four-star system. Design something that works for you and will facilitate any dialogue you may have with those with whom you are sharing your statements. Refine your statement to reflect a good mix of attributes that are already established, in process, and just beginning to emerge.

HOW WILL YOU MANIFEST YOUR IDENTITY?

After you have an initial group of statements, consider how they are meant to manifest. Is there a particular job, activity, people group, or passion of yours that you can specifically identify? Below are a few ideas inspired from a variety of the Identity Statements I've collected from different friends. These statements are sharp, targeted, free of flowery phrases, and express the how, where, or who of the identity of these people:

I am a beholder of a majestic God—an accurate image of His goodness.

I am true to the meaning of my name. I am one who gathers through friendship and administrative communication.

I am a deep thinker, a lover of wisdom and the ways of God, a father of process as a key to a powerful life.

I am a trainer who instills new ideas through imagination and creativity. I awaken dormant passions through innovative teaching that impacts businesses, families, marriages, careers, and relationships with God.

I am the beloved of God, one who sings with all my heart the songs He has sung over me.

I am an anointed mother pouring out love, kindness, compassion, and wisdom into my own children and also to others.

I am a joyful promise keeper who holds on to the promises of God and keeps her promises to others.

I am a wise-hearted creator of artistic workmanship of beauty that reflects God's glory. I mix sounds, images, and words into vivid expressions of the Father's heart for Christians and pre-Christians.

I am an author of enduring words that bring freedom from religious slavery.

I am His delightful son, confident in my place in the family. Through friendship, I impart the confidence of His unfailing love to those who have yet to discover it.

I am a teacher and a writer who creates bridges between concepts and realities for people to cross over from their potential to their actual destiny.

I am a warrior who relishes the fight, a lover of majesty who promotes the power of the one with the One—developing and empowering a new breed of warriors.

I am heaven's storyteller of hope, faith and love to the earth. In every-day conversations, I bring God's lenses of possibilities for those who see only problems.

I am a leader who identifies and empowers the treasure in others, enabling them to rise as Kingdom warriors of strength and joy.

I release rivers of financial blessing that flow to my friends, family, and ministries. I create and funnel finances into Kingdom initiatives.

I am a resource of God's wisdom to those around me, freely giving away what my Father has given to me.

I am a releaser of His joy and peace—a carrier of the refreshing Spirit of God into battle. When I walk into a war-weary room, atmospheres are changed from tired to renewed.

I am God's much-loved son, in whom He is well pleased. People hear His words in my words.

SHARING AND DECLARING

Sharing your Identity Statement or even reading it aloud to yourself can feel a bit awkward at first. This is very common because you are doing something that you may not have done before. Often, there is still a lens that declaring your identity feels self-centered or self-promoting, but when we live with God's true perspective of humility, we can rejoice that while we know who we are without Him, we're also discovering who we are with Him!

There's usually a gap between your potential and your actual that will be in many of your statements—and that's okay. That is where saying, "I am and am becoming . . ." works really well. It reflects the thought I've heard expressed by several of my favorite teachers: "I may not yet be where I will be, but thank God, I'm not where I used to be!" It is indeed a process of maturity, and that is understood.

But even if it feels a bit strange, go for it anyway! Reading your Identity Statements aloud connects to your spirit and will begin to renew your mind. There's something powerful about putting our vocal chords to words. It's a great part of the process to grow through and is worth doing. God delights in who He created you to be. Enjoy engaging with Him in that celebration.

Eventually, if you are going on this journey with a group of friends, take the plunge and share some of your Identity Statements with each other. It is a huge source of support and encouragement to rejoice over each other in this process; and when you forget who you are momentarily, your friends get to come alongside you and remind you kindly of who you really are.

In the communities that I am a part of, we all have a copy of our Identity Statements and use them regularly for prayer and processing our lives together. When we update them, those we are in close partnership with get updates. We use them to pray for each other and express encouragement. Sharing and dialoguing identity can be a powerful accelerant to relationships and development in any community you are a part of. It's probably been the most significant tool we've used in mentoring and training for fostering relational connections and friendships.

CONNECTING YOUR PROMISES

As we said before, your promises are your currency and resource for your identity. Every aspect of your identity will have promises connected to them. Look for scriptures or other promises God has given you that specifically speak to this aspect of your identity. Some may be a resource for more than one aspect of your identity.

When that part of your identity is under fire, few things are more powerful than pulling out your promises and saying, "Lord, You said . . ." Of course, it's not with your hand on your hip, wagging your finger in His face—but with the absolute conviction of His true nature of faithfulness to His word. "I know You, and I know what You have promised." It's a powerful way to pray.

UPGRADING AND REFINING

In the beginning, your initial statements may only last a month or so. My first collection of Identity Statements was five pages long! I had poured in every scripture, observation and promise for an entire lifetime, wanting to value them all. I had some serious refining to do, but I still remember the delight God had that I was taking the plunge. Thanks to some good friends who understood that I had no training, just loads of enthusiasm, I began to refine it down into something far sharper and more targeted. So the first version of my Identity Statement lasted about 16 days.

Change and refine it as often as you like. I would suggest keeping all the various forms it appears in. I know mine serve as an interesting source of evidence of transformation on my journey with God. I have a notebook that holds all the versions, and it serves as a collection spot for items I haven't fully processed yet.

After the dust settles, revisit your Identity Statement every few months or when circumstances dictate. Have you come into a new level of maturity that requires an update to your identity? Often, the source of our struggles and insecurities is that the revelation of our identity in Christ, and who He plans to be for us, has not been adequately updated for the new opportunity or battle we're currently engaged in.

Simply remember that there are no hard and fast rules. Create a process that is living, powerful, and has meaning for you. Allow for growth and refinement. Maintain a sense of joy and expectancy at all times, as well as the wonder that even this is just a small glimpse of the magnificent, expansive, gracious view of the image that God sees when He looks at you.

WHO DOES GOD SAY THAT YOU ARE?

In addition to the scriptures that we refer to as Inheritance Words, there is a wealth of scripture that describes who God sees us to be. While we can enjoy collecting the clues to our true identity, there is tremendous power in times of meditation and declaration of God's Word.

Create a list of scriptures that describe who the Father created you to be in Christ. Here are a few to get you started:

I am a new creation:
2 Corinthians 5:17—"Therefore, if anyone is in Christ, he is a new creation; old things have passed away; behold, all things have become new."

As Jesus is, so am I in this life:
1 John 4:17—". . . as He is, so are we in this world."

I am Accepted in the Beloved—accepted completely and totally by God in Christ:
Ephesians 1:6—". . . to the praise of the glory of His grace, by which He made us accepted in the Beloved."

I am a chosen one, part of a chosen generation—a special man or woman of God:
1 Peter 2:9—"But you are a chosen generation, a royal priesthood, a holy nation, His own special people, that you may proclaim the praises of Him who called you out of darkness into His marvelous light."

I am a friend of Jesus:
John 15:15—"No longer do I call you servants, for a servant does not know what his master is doing; but I have called you friends, for all things that I heard from My Father I have made known to you."

I am beautifully crafted by God, designed for good works already prepared by Him: Ephesians 2:10—"For we are His workmanship, created in Christ Jesus for good works, which God prepared beforehand that we should walk in them."

I am wonderfully known by God and beautifully made by Him: Psalms 139:1, 14—"O Lord, You have searched me and known me . . . I am fearfully and wonderfully made."

The list could go on and on.[x] Allow the Holy Spirit to highlight, expand, and custom tailor these scriptures for you. Some may become inheritance words for you; others will begin to seep down into your soul and renew your mind as to who you really are in the eyes and heart of God.

Choose some favorites and pair them with a photograph that reflects your identity. Write them in your own words. Enjoy the conversation with the Holy Spirit as to how He personally sees these types of scriptures when He looks at you. Record your thoughts in a journal or notebook containing your identity explorations, and delight in the image God sees of you.

Evidences of Transformation

In a lifestyle of process, we use Evidences of Transformation instead of assessments of comprehension of materials. It is important to be good Bereans (Acts 17:11) in our learning, but everything we learn must be accompanied by a living experience with the Author of that truth. Otherwise, it's just something we know, not Someone we've encountered. And as has been said many times throughout this book, beholding and becoming (2 Corinthians 3:18) is the most powerful key to unlocking The Image—the image of Christ in us.

When knowledge has been combined with personal experience, there will be evidences of that in how we perceive, think, speak, and act. Each area should have a statement of the transformation you've encountered, as well as a real-world story that exemplifies it.

So, what are your initial Evidences of Transformation since you began interacting with *The Image*?

Then, return to these every few months and consider how you are continuing to grow up into all things in Christ.

And when you finish your first Evidences of Transformation, sit back and take some time to reflect on who God has been for you as you've been reading.

Begin to dream with Him about who you are becoming and what is possible now.

EVIDENCES OF TRANSFORMATION

PERCEPTION—How we see ourselves, others and the world around us

1. Perception of God
"Instead of seeing God as . . . I now see Him much more as . . ."

Share an occasion where you saw this occur:

2. Perception of yourself
"Previously, I perceived that I was . . ."
"Now, I see myself more as . . ."

Share a story of when you saw this evidence of transformation in how you perceived yourself:

MINDSETS—How we think about our perceptions

1. Thinking about God

What are some of the new, brilliant thoughts you are now having about the true nature of God?

Share a story about how an old way of thinking about God has upgraded to a new, more accurate mindset about who He really is:

2. Thinking about yourself

Write a one sentence description of who you see yourself to be in Christ:

How is this different than what you would have said before reading *The Image*?

Share a story that exemplifies greater kindness and grace you are experiencing in how you think about yourself:

LANGUAGE—How we speak about God, ourselves and others

1. Talking about God

What are some of the descriptive words you find yourself using to talk about God?

2. Talking about ourselves

How has your language about yourself transformed? What are you saying (or not saying) that is an evidence of that?

3. How you speak about others

What areas of transformation have you seen in how you speak about friends, family, and those you encounter in your daily life?

Share a real-life example of a transformation in how you speak about God, yourself, or others that is a good example of this:

ACTIONS—How your new ways of thinking and perceiving have translated into behavior

1. How has your daily behavior been impacted by your new perceptions and mindsets? What are you doing now that you've not done before?

Share a story of a new response or behavior that was inspired by your experience with *The Image:*

ADDITIONAL RESOURCES

The following resources are available for further exploration at **www.BrilliantBookHouse.com.**

Allison Bown
>   **Books:**
>   *Joyful Intentionality: A Passion-filled Life on Purpose*
>
>   **CD series:**
>   *Unpacking Your True Identity*
>   *Secrets of a Spiritual Warrior*
>   *Conversations with God*

Graham Cooke
>   **Books:**
>   *The Nature of God*
>   *The Language of Promise*
>   *Beholding and Becoming*
>   *Letters from God: The Nature of Freedom*
>   *Letters from God: Newness of Life*
>   *Corporate Prophetic Words*
>
>   **CD series:**
>   *Living in Your Truest Identity*
>   *Maintaining Your Inner Compass*
>   *Defining Your Personal Legacy*
>   *Cultivating the Fruit of the Spirit*
>
>   **Devotional Soaking:**
>   *Becoming the Beloved*

END NOTES
FOR THE IMAGE

Prologue

i   Ansel Adams, *Examples: The Making of 40 photographs* (Little, Brown; New Ed edition1989)

Introduction:

ii Paul Froese and Christopher Bader, *America's Four Gods: What We Say about God--and What That Says about Us* (New York: Oxford Press University Press, 2010)

Chapter 2

iii Williamson, Marianne. *A Return to Love: Reflections on the Principles of "A Course in Miracles" (HarperOne, 1996)*

Chapter 6

iv *Secretariat,* directed by Randall Wallace (Disney, 2010)

Part II

Introduction

v   The term "Brilliant community" refers to Brilliant Perspectives (www.Brilliant-Perspectives.com). Brilliant Book House (www.BrilliantBookHouse.com), and Brilliant (TV www.BrilliantTV.com)

Identity Clues—Inheritance Words

vi For more on Inheritance Words, read "Processing Inheritance Words" in my book *Joyful Intentionality.*

Identity Clues—God's Words to You

vii For more on corporate prophetic words, read my book "But I Don't Have a Prophetic Word" in *Joyful Intentionality*

Identity Clues—Who Are Your Heroes?

viii Graham Cooke, *Qualities of a Spiritual Warrior*, Way of the Warrior, (Brilliant Book House, 2008).

Identity Clues—Ideas from Fellow Travelers

ix *Apollo 13*, directed by Ron Howard (Imagine Entertainment, 1995)

Who Does God Say That You Are?

x For more on who you are in Christ, listen to Graham Cooke's "Session 6: Capturing the Thoughts of God", *Mind of a Saint* (Brilliant Book House, 2013). In it Cooke gives a list of your standing in Christ with over 100 scriptural statements of who you are in Christ. It is available on CD at www.BrilliantBookHouse.com or streaming video at www.BrilliantTV.com.

ABOUT THE AUTHOR

As an author, international speaker, consultant, trainer and strategist, Allison Bown has worked in a variety of roles over the past decade in partnership with Graham Cooke. Together, they have developed teaching and training for people to discover the passion that God has for them and how it becomes part of their everyday experience.

After an initial career in psychology, Allison moved to Yosemite National Park in the early 1980s with her husband Randy and worked at The Ansel Adams Gallery for several years as an office manager and photographic workshop director, continuing a tradition of collaborative photography programs that began in 1940. She later became an educator and spent 20 wonderful years at Yosemite National Park El Portal School. During this time, she also ministered weekly to inmates in central California's prisons and jails with Aglow Prison Ministry and trained leaders for APM across the state.

Allison left education to join Graham Cooke in developing a number of initiatives, including prophetic intercession and fresh, relational ways to train and develop people in their life with God. She currently works with Graham as a Creative Partner for Brilliant, developing teaching, coaching and support for the growing Brilliant TV community. She has a regular blog on the Brilliant Perspectives website and published her first book, *Joyful Intentionality* with Brilliant Book House.

When she's not writing or collaborating, Allison can likely be found hiking in a Sequoia grove near her hometown in the Sierra Nevada foothills with Randy or walking along the beach in Santa Barbara. She divides her time between these two lovely locations, enjoying a marvelous community of family and friends in each one.